A Deep Study of Character

Lucy Calkins, Series Editor

Mary Ehrenworth

Photography by Peter Cunningham

Illustrations by Marjorie Martinelli

HEINEMANN ◆ PORTSMOUTH, NH

For Marc Todd, whose character has shaped a generation of students.

Heinemann
361 Hanover Street
Portsmouth, NH 03801–3912
www.heinemann.com

Offices and agents throughout the world

© 2017 by Mary Ehrenworth and Lucy Calkins

All rights reserved. No part of this book may be reproduced in any form or by any electronic or mechanical means, including information storage and retrieval systems, without permission in writing from the publisher, except by a reviewer, who may quote brief passages in a review, with the exception of reproducible pages, which are identified by the *A Deep Study of Character* copyright line and can be photocopied for classroom use only.

> *The author has dedicated a great deal of time and effort to writing the content of this book, and her written expression is protected by copyright law. We respectfully ask that you do not adapt, reuse, or copy anything on third-party (whether for-profit or not-for-profit) lesson-sharing websites. As always, we're happy to answer any questions you may have.*
>
> —Heinemann Publishers

"Dedicated to Teachers" is a trademark of Greenwood Publishing Group, Inc.

The author and publisher wish to thank those who have generously given permission to reprint borrowed material:

Excerpts from *First French Kiss* by Adam Bagdasarian (Farrar, Straus and Giroux, 2005). Used by permission of Oracle Associates, literary agent.

"Thank You, M'am" from *Short Stories* by Langston Hughes. Copyright © 1996 by Ramona Bass and Arnold Rampersad. Reprinted by permission of Hilland Wang, a division of Farrar, Straus and Giroux and by permission of Harold Ober Associates Incorporated.

Cataloging-in-Publication data is on file with the Library of Congress.

ISBN-13: 978-0-325-09723-7

Editor: Karen Kawaguchi
Production: Elizabeth Valway
Cover and interior designs: Jenny Jensen Greenleaf
Photography: Peter Cunningham and David Stirling
Illustrations: Marjorie Martinelli
Composition: Publishers' Design and Production Services, Inc.
Manufacturing: Steve Bernier

Printed in the United States of America on acid-free paper
21 20 19 18 VP   3 4 5

Contents

Acknowledgments • vi

An Orientation to the Unit • vii

BEND I Considering Complex Character Traits

Letter to Teachers—Day Zero • 5
Today you'll remind students to use what they know about choosing books wisely to get themselves quickly into books. You'll also use your assessment data and knowledge of books and students to make specific recommendations.

1. Read-Aloud: Investigating Multiple Character Traits • 10
Today you'll read aloud the first half of "Popularity" by Adam Bagdasarian, from First French Kiss. You will teach students that subtle details can suggest a lot of information about a character, especially about their traits.

2. Readers Revise Their Thinking as They Accumulate Evidence • 20
Today you'll teach students that characters reveal themselves over time, and that readers must remain alert to new details and be willing to rethink their initial ideas. You'll demonstrate this in the read-aloud text, showing kids how you can make a theory chart that shows evidence of (and revision of) your theories.

3. Developing Courses of Study with a Partner: Book Choices and Thinking Work • 30
Today you'll remind students that readers' thinking about characters is influenced by the genre they are reading, or the course of study they are on.

4. Perceptive Readers Acknowledge the Parts of a Character that Are Less Likeable • 34
Today you'll teach students that though it's easy to sympathize with and defend characters, perceptive readers realize that like real people, characters are complex and have less likeable parts.

5. Read-Aloud: Some Character Traits Matter More Than Others, Because They Affect the Rest of the Story • 40
Today you'll read aloud the second half of "Popularity" by Adam Bagdasarian, from First French Kiss. You will teach students that readers begin to realize that some character traits matter more than others, because they affect what happens in the rest of the story.

6. Lifting the Level of Your Writing about Reading • 49
Today you'll teach students several tips to help them lift the level of their writing about reading.

7. Readers Consider the Pressures Acting on Characters • 56
Today you'll teach students to consider pressures on characters that might cause them to behave in less-than-likeable ways. Readers do this by returning to scenes where the behavior emerges and analyzing possible causes.

8. Readers Reflect (on Their Novels and Their Reading Lives) • 64
Today you could teach students that at the end of novels, readers reflect back on the story and the characters, with perspective gained from finishing the book.

BEND II Investigating How Setting Shapes Characters

9. Read-Aloud: Characters Are Often Shaped by the Mood or Atmosphere of the Setting • 72

Today you'll use your read-aloud of the first half of "The Fight" by Adam Bagdasarian to teach students that even when the setting is the sort they are apt to overlook because it seems ordinary, it can affect characters deeply. You'll highlight the importance of a setting's mood.

10. Readers Attend to the Precise Language Authors Use to Describe the Setting • 82

Today you'll teach your students that when readers think about how the setting influences characters, they pay attention to the author's specific language. This helps readers to grasp the mood, atmosphere, norms, and tempo of a place—all of which can matter in deep and hidden ways to a character.

11. Sometimes Characters Are Torn by Competing Pressures, Including the Pressures of a Place • 89

Today you'll teach your students that one way to investigate the relationship between the setting and characters is to pay attention to inconsistencies between characters' behaviors and their inner thinking. When characters are torn and inconsistencies arise, it could be that external pressures from their surroundings led them away from their inner compass.

12. Settings Can Change over Time, Not Just Physically, but Psychologically • 96

Today you'll teach your students that the setting in a story can keep changing not just physically, but psychologically. Readers trace the setting over time, investigating how the place changes, and how it affects characters differently in different moments.

13. Read-Aloud: Characters Acting as a Group Can Wield Enormous Influence, for Good or for Evil • 104

Today you'll read aloud the second half of your text (we read from "The Fight" from First French Kiss). You'll teach students that in addition to places affecting characters, characters can also act as positive or negative forces on a place.

14. Settings Also Change in Time, Often Bringing in Backstory to Develop the Character • 113

Today you'll teach students that settings may change in terms of time, often bringing in backstory to develop the character. Perceptive readers are alert to these time changes and how they give the reader added insight into the character.

15. Readers Share Their Work and Reflect on Their Challenges and Growth • 119

Today you could teach students that readers look for ways to reflect on how they are becoming more powerful thinkers, and that one window into their thinking will be the writing they do about reading.

BEND III Analyzing Characters as Vehicles for Themes

16. Read-Aloud: Characters' Troubles Become Motifs in a Story • 125

Today you'll teach, through a read-aloud in which you channel students to study a video alongside you, that perceptive readers explore motifs in stories, often by analyzing the troubles characters face, and considering how these conflicts become subjects or motifs in a story.

17. Moving from Motifs to Themes • 135

Today you'll teach students that by studying what an author has to say about a motif, readers can start to develop ideas about themes.

18. Investigating How Symbolism Relates to Themes • 142

Today you'll teach students that authors often layer symbolism in narratives, and that these symbols are often related to significant themes. Readers consider how symbols relate to or develop an important theme.

19. Taking Charge of Your Collaborative Reading Life • 148

Today you'll teach students that partners can take charge of their collaborative reading lives by considering what's worth working on together, then making sure their writing about reading and talk reflect that focus. You'll teach students to lean on each other, support each other, and push each other.

20. Read-Aloud: Reading Aloud to Support Repertoire and Agency • 155
Today you'll encourage readers to make choices and draw flexibly on a range of reading skills during a read-aloud of "Thank You, M'am" by Langston Hughes.

21. Reflection and Agency Centers • 165
Today you could invite your students to move through centers that are set up to invite reflection and agency.

 Registration instructions to access the digital resources that accompany this book may be found on p. xi.

Acknowledgments

WHEN YOU WORK with witty, wise, irreverent colleagues, and among teachers who love books and kids, every part of what you do is informed by their words and their work. I can imagine middle school teachers from Seattle to Barcelona to New York seeing their influence in these pages. I can hear in my mind the conversations with staff developers who have long left TCRWP, and those I spoke with at Teachers College yesterday. I know that all of the literacy work we invent is invented collaboratively, through workshops and conferences, work in classrooms, and over glasses of wine. To my colleagues at Teachers College and in schools, and especially to the Middle School Team at TCRWP, thank you for all of those conversations, for sharing student work, and for caring so much about reading.

There are a few people whose thinking has particularly influenced the work in this book. I adore the work that Chris Lehman and Kate Roberts did in *Falling in Love with Close Reading*, and you'll see references to their work, especially to teaching students to read with specific lenses, in this unit of study on character. A number of my colleagues have been writing their own units of study for this middle school series. In particular, Audra Robb, Katy Wischow, and Katie Clements have proven to be some of my most invaluable thought partners as we've read each other's work and piloted lessons together. I can't say enough about the love and gratitude I have for these women, who gave so generously of their time and and ideas to help make this unit its strongest.

In the schools, there have been some incredible practitioners whose structures, or student work, or ways of teaching, or rituals with students around reading, are brought to life here. They include Stacey Fell and Carole Mashamesh at Tompkins Square Middle School, Heather Freyman, Christina DiZebba, and Marc Todd at IS 289, Tim Sorensen at Middlesex Middle School, Elisa Zonana and Mark Federman at East Side Community High School, and Marcie von Beck of Thurgood Marshall Elementary.

Thank you to the team at Heinemann Publishing, who make books like these possible, so that we can help teachers help their students. Anna Gratz Cockerille was the developmental and content editor, and also a real thought and writing partner, and I hope to write many more books with her. Anna's attentiveness and grace kept it all going and made writing a pleasure, and her contributions are integral to the final book. Karen Kawaguchi edited and, as usual, helped bring the book beautifully into production, where it was cared for by Shannon Thorner and Elizabeth Valway. Editorial director and program manager Abby Heim, and marketing director Lisa Bingen, believed in and advocated for these middle school units of study.

Finally, there is Lucy Calkins. Lucy makes all of our work possible at TCRWP. She pushes herself harder than anybody, she questions everything, and she creates tremendous opportunities, for me, for my colleagues, and for the teachers we care so much about. And not only this, Lucy takes an active role in the development of each and every book in each and every series. No unit book, including this one, would be what it is without her feedback, her partnership, and her support on round after round of revision. Thank you.

An Orientation to the Unit

THIS UNIT IS FOR TEACHERS whose students could grow as readers through a deep study of character. They'll grow by learning to consider more complex character traits, to investigate how setting shapes characters, and to analyze how characters are vehicles for themes. It's also for teachers whose readers need to take more charge of their reading lives, so that they read more, they annotate and jot in ways that deepen their thinking, and they hold smart literary conversations with other readers.

The unit is also a kind of a primer in what it means to participate in an intense reading workshop. It introduces students to a variety of instructional methods, and coaches both teachers and readers how to harness those methods to increase expertise and independence. One method will be instructional read-aloud. This is not "pack and snack" read-aloud, nor is it "play the audible version with the famous actor," nor is it "listen to the teacher think aloud." It is a lively, fast-paced method aimed at engaging students immediately in raising the level of their reading work. Your thought prompts will be planned and strategic. Partner conversation will be responsive to these prompts. You'll listen carefully to kids, with possible feedback in mind, and you'll habituate your students to getting feedback from you, and applying that feedback to their work immediately. This process intensifies the relationship between teaching and learning, teaches students to attend to you and to stories, and gets as close as you can to 100% engagement, 100% of the time.

You'll notice that during read-aloud, there is virtually no all-class conversation, and instead readers talk often and briefly in partnerships, and you summarize what they say and move forward. These techniques aim to maintain the intense pace of the read-aloud. They also aim to give each and every reader lots of oral practice of academic discussion. Kids learn academic discourse by *practicing* academic discourse. In the read-aloud, then, they'll listen to you and the story, they'll talk intensely with each other, they'll hear you repeat some of what was said and give additional tips for ways to raise the level of their thinking, and they'll do this work in repeated rounds.

The focus on partner discussion and partner work is intense across this unit, and you'll find that there is curriculum embedded for partnerships. Learning to be an effective study partner will give students academic capital. You'll teach those skills across this unit. That means you want to put some thought (with your students) into forming partnerships, and revise and renegotiate them as needed. There is more in *A Guide to the Reading Workshop: Middle School Grades* on setting up partnerships. For now, consider reading levels, interest in particular genres, social dynamics, and reading habits. The goal is for partnerships to challenge each other, and to support each other in extending their powers.

Another instructional method that you want to get more and more skilled at (it's a never-ending process) will be teaching reading minilessons. You'll see that the connections in these minilessons are brief, and often, you'll ask students to get out their homework from the night before (usually a combination of reading, thinking, jotting) and share it with a partner. That decision is deliberate, as is the decision to give specific homework each night. We know that for kids to succeed in high school, they have to be able to do homework. Kids who can get high-level thinking and reading work done outside of school will do better in every discipline. So you might want to review homework sections as you preview the minilessons.

In the minilesson, most of the time, you teach a reading strategy and demonstrate it in the story that was read aloud. Then the students practice the work briefly, either in a different section of the read-aloud text, or in their own books. Every now and then, instead of returning to the read-aloud text, the minilesson invites you and your students to practice the work using a video, often a YouTube clip of a popular film. Sometimes videos work perfectly in terms of engaging students quickly in high-level work, and moving quickly across parts of a story. When you get to the link of the minilesson, notice how you almost always review the work that kids have been doing and invite them to add this new strategy to their repertoire. Then you have them plan their work quickly with a partner, before going off to read. All this attention to methods aims to produce kids who know how to attend to instruction, to apply work they've tried in a lesson or read-aloud to their own text, and to work with a partner to make a reading plan and strive to achieve it.

OVERVIEW

Bend I: Considering Complex Character Traits

Bend I teaches readers to analyze complex character traits, including thinking about how some character traits emerge across a narrative, how readers collect evidence to support their thinking about character traits, and how readers revise their thinking in the face of new evidence. The characters in the novels students are reading are complicated, and this bend not only pushes students toward more rigorous, text-based analysis, it also pushes students to examine sides of characters that readers often ignore, such as their less likeable parts. Readers also consider the pressures that are exerted on characters—what makes them the way they are. At the end of the bend, readers reflect on insights they gleaned about characters that they might apply to their own lives—to the people in their lives and to themselves.

Meanwhile across Bend I, readers also learn to listen carefully to spoken language in the read-aloud, engage in literary conversation and increasingly academic discourse in partner discussion, begin to annotate and jot as they read, and use a reading notebook to capture and develop their best thinking. They'll also embark on "courses of study," which means a few books that they choose with a partner and read together. If you have enough books for partners to read the same titles, that's fabulous. If not, they can read the same genre, or same author, or same series. The main thing is, readers learn to choose a few books at a time, for the purpose of moving their reading lives forward. They'll also keep records of what they read, on paper or in digital reading logs such as calendars, apps, or lists—simple tools that will help them reflect on their overall reading volume over time. This bend will take about ten days to two weeks, and students will try to read two novels in that time.

Bend II: Investigating How Setting Shapes Characters

Bend II asks students to keep doing the character trait analysis work they learned in Bend I and introduces new work of investigating the intersection of setting and characters. Your readers already know how to identify a setting, and some will have thought about how the setting affects characters. Now you'll teach them to think about the mood, or atmosphere of a setting, and the specific language the author uses to evoke that atmosphere. You'll teach students to think of setting as a psychological force, and to investigate how it influences characters, as well as how group dynamics and individuals influence the psychology of a place.

Meanwhile, you'll increase the expectations for students' reading volume and for their agency in doing homework, both reading and jotting. Readers will aim, by Bend II, to read for thirty to forty minutes at night, and they will try to read, by the end of the bend, thirty to forty pages each night, taking more time to read as needed. They'll take serious time at the end of the bend to reflect on their reading lives with a partner, thinking about what is going well, how they are growing, and how they might solve problems and meet challenges. Students should be on their third and fourth novels in this bend.

Bend III: Analyzing Characters as Vehicles for Themes

Bend III moves students to investigating how characters act as vehicles for themes in novels. You'll teach readers to consider the troubles characters face as possible motifs, or subjects the author is preoccupied with, and to find passages in their novels where these motifs appear. Then, readers will begin to question the text more deeply, asking what the author suggests about these motifs, and developing possible thematic statements. As in Bends I and II, you'll push readers to ground their theories in specific text evidence. Once readers have a few themes they are tracing in their novels, you'll introduce the notion that often, authors use interesting craft, such as symbolism, to develop these themes. You'll invite your readers to explore symbolism and how it might relate to theme.

Meanwhile, you'll increase expectations for independence, asking students to set their own homework using your anchor charts, their knowledge of genre, and their partner as a study support. The bend ends with a repertoire read-aloud, in which you invite students to review the reading work they know how to do, and to read a fresh story with you, with students in charge of the reading work. The goal is to lead readers to realize that stories suggest certain kinds of thinking at certain points. Finally, you end with a day of reflection and agency centers, where students reflect on their growth and apply what they've learned. Across the unit, most readers will read four to six novels.

GETTING READY

There are a few things to do to get ready for this unit. You will see, at the beginning of Bend I, a "Day Zero." This session helps you to quickly get students into books, pair them up, even informally, as partners, and have them begin to keep some kind of record of what they read. Of course, there is a lot more to say about all of those moves, and you can read more specifically about assessing readers, establishing partnerships, matching kids to books, and using reading logs to reflect on volume in *A Guide to the Reading Workshop: Middle School Grades*. Here are a few big-picture items to consider as you prepare for the unit.

Marking Up and Rehearsing the Read-Aloud

There are three read-aloud texts that anchor the instruction across the unit, one for each bend. The first two are stories from a short story collection, and the third is a digital narrative that is a music video. Read-aloud, as described previously, is intense and strategic in this unit. You'll want to take a few minutes and jot some Post-its® for yourself, and stick them on the story, with the prompts you will give students, what you will listen for in their partner talk, and some predictable feedback, usually in the form of tips.

This instructional work is embedded in the text of the read-aloud sessions. I've also included a copy of my read-aloud text, with my notes for read-aloud, in the online resources as an example. A little bit of preparation and rehearsal will help you focus on what students say during read-aloud, rather than on what you'll say.

The read-aloud texts are:

- "Popularity" by Adam Bagdasarian, from *First French Kiss*
- "The Fight" by Adam Bagdasarian, from *First French Kiss*

- "You Belong with Me," a music video by Taylor Swift. A link to the video is provided in the online resources.
- "Thank You, M'am" by Langston Hughes

What Kids Will Read: Partner Books and Courses of Study

The only things that matter about the books kids are reading in this unit is that readers choose them, readers love them, and the books are at the outer edge of readers' zone of proximal development. Here's why these things matter. Choice matters because it leads to increased engagement. Engagement leads to increased achievement. That they love their books matters because one goal of the unit is to get kids to read more. So you want them in books that make kids want to read. Fortunately, young adult (YA) literature is thriving, and there are hordes of titles that turn kids into readers. You can read more about libraries, titles, and teen readers in *A Guide to the Reading Workshop: Middle School Grades* and in information about the Teachers College Reading and Writing Project (TCRWP) Classroom Libraries. That the books are at kids' outer edge of proximal development matters because you are not only striving to get kids to read more, you also are striving to move them up text levels, so they are able to read increasingly complex novels with interest, ease, and expertise.

In this unit of study, right from the start, students get a reading partner, and together, partners embark on "courses of study." Essentially, this means a few books that readers choose together, at one time, that go together and will move readers forward. For instance, if partners have been reading a lot of John Green, and they're ready for some slightly harder novels about intense relationships, loss, and emotional drama, they might choose some Jodi Picoult novels, or a mix of Green followed by Picoult. Another partnership, reading below grade level, wants to read fantasy. These partners want to (or you want them to) work hard at reading a lot and moving up levels, so they might choose the Spiderwick Chronicles series, with a tentative plan to follow those up with the Deltora Quest series.

If you have enough paired titles, or you can inspire your students to get books on devices, used or new books, and library books, then partners can read the same titles, which is lovely. It is also perfectly fine for them to swap books, reading books in the same series but not the same exact titles, or reading in the same author or genre. The real point is that they are embarking on some shared work together as study partners. That means partners need to more or less read at similar levels and have similar interests.

Preview the Pacing of Sessions

The real reason to preview the sessions is so that you have in your mind a kind of pacing calendar. Ultimately, you'll probably want to move these sessions onto an actual calendar, so you have start and end dates for the unit, and you can mark which days you'll be doing read-aloud and which days you'll be teaching a minilesson, and what text you need for each day. You might want to also mark if there are any charts or tools that you might need, and print those from the online resources. Some of these tools will be for the conferring and small-group work, and if you have the tools printed out and in a folder, you're probably more likely to teach those small groups.

The read-alouds are divided across two days, so you can read these stories and engage in partner talk, across two forty- to forty-five-minute periods. You'll find that the read-aloud days are not sequential. Rather, you read the beginning of a story, then teach a couple of minilessons using the first half—often strategies that lead readers to preliminary theories. Then you read the rest of the story and teach minilessons using the second half—often strategies on revising and complicating theories in the face of new text.

The shares of each session are usually matched to the homework, and the homework is often used in the following day's minilesson. You might want to glance at these and add a note to your pacing calendar.

Following is a Read-Aloud Pacing Guide to help you plan your sessions.

READ-ALOUD PACING GUIDE

BEND I	**Read-Aloud Text: "Popularity"** by Adam Bagdasarian, from *First French Kiss*
Session 1 Read-Aloud	Read aloud the first half of the story, until the end of the line, "I did not know then that popularity has a life span, and that Mitch's time was about to run out."
Session 2	Revisit an excerpt from the first half of story.
Session 3	
Session 4	Show a short video clip from *Harry Potter and the Half-Blood Prince*.
Session 5 Read-Aloud	Read aloud the second half of the story.
Session 6	
Session 7	Revisit a short video clip from *Harry Potter and the Half-Blood Prince*. Revisit an excerpt from the second half of the story.
Session 8	
BEND II	**Read-Aloud Text: "The Fight"** by Adam Bagdasarian, from *First French Kiss*
Session 9 Read-Aloud	Read aloud the first half of the story, until the end of the line, "It would be a fight to some extreme and horrifying limit—a fight to unconsciousness or hospitalization or reconstructive surgery."
Session 10	Revisit an excerpt from the first half of the story.
Session 11	Revisit an excerpt from the first half of the story.
Session 12	Show a video clip from *Stranger Things*. Revisit excerpts from the "Popularity" and "The Fight."

Session 13 Read-Aloud	Read aloud the second half of "The Fight."
Session 14	Show two video clips, "Potions Class at Hogwarts" and "Severus Snape: Important Scenes in Chronological Order." Display, annotate, and discuss an excerpt from "One Holy Night" by Sandra Cisneros, from *Woman Hollering Creek*.
Session 15	
BEND III	**Video Text: "You Belong with Me,"** narrative music video by Taylor Swift **Read-Aloud Text: "Thank You, M'am"** by Langston Hughes
Session 16 Read-Aloud	Read aloud/video "You Belong with Me"
Session 17	Revisit parts of "You Belong with Me"
Session 18	Revisit parts of "You Belong with Me"
Session 19	
Session 20 Read-Aloud	Read aloud "Thank You, M'am" by Langston Hughes
Session 21	

ONLINE DIGITAL RESOURCES

A variety of resources to accompany this unit of study are available in the online resources, including charts and examples of student work shown throughout *A Deep Study of Character*, as well as links to other electronic resources. Offering daily support for your teaching, these materials will help you provide a structured learning environment that fosters independence and self-direction.

To access and download all the digital resources for *A Deep Study of Character*:

1. Go to www.heinemann.com and click the link in the upper right to log in. (If you do not have an account yet, you will need to create one.)

2. Enter the following registration code in the box to register your product: MSRUOS_GHAQ5.

3. Enter the security information requested.

4. Once you have registered your product it will appear in the list of My Online Resources.

(You may keep copies of these resources on up to six of your own computers or devices. By downloading the file you acknowledge that they are for your individual or classroom use and that neither the resources nor the product code will be distributed or shared.)

Considering Complex Character Traits BEND I

A Letter to Teachers

Dear Teachers,

Welcome to a deep study of character! Readers love to study characters, and characters reward deep study. Whether you are thinking hard about Katniss or about Anna Karenina, it's fascinating to ponder characters' strengths and flaws, why they do the things they do, and the parts of them that change. We have to wait so long in our own lives to see the people around us change. Children have to wait so long to feel like they are growing up. But characters in novels change and grow across the pages, and we can see and study the drama of their lives in even a few days of reading.

The unit has a few big goals. First and foremost, is to help students take charge of their reading lives with zeal. Another goal is to lead teen readers to pay closer attention to detail in their novels, especially details about characters that suggest the ways that characters are complicated. A third goal is to teach students to develop more nuanced thinking about the role that setting, especially the psychology of the setting, plays in shaping the characters. A fourth goal is to help readers think about the relationship between the conflicts characters face and the themes that are developed in the novel.

We'll begin in Bend I to investigate character traits. Students have thought about character traits since they were in first or second grade, of course. What gets ever-more fascinating for teens is how the characters in the novels they are reading become more complicated. It takes longer to get to know them. They are slower to reveal themselves, much like their teen readers. Some of their mistakes or less likeable traits, which may have simply seemed unpleasant, become significant because they shape what happens to other people. It's all tremendously interesting.

Interwoven with the minilessons in this book are read-aloud sessions. The goal of read-aloud is to introduce a series of reading skills or strategies to demonstrate multiple reading skills being used at once. The read-aloud models reading in action, flexibly attending to the reading work the text calls for. On a read-aloud day, you'll give students specific lenses to listen with as you read, and you'll interrupt the story for specific, related, turn-and-talk conversations. Occasionally you'll give feedback to students on their reading work, or demonstrate. Expect that your read-aloud sessions will take about twenty to twenty-five minutes, and that students will only have ten or fifteen minutes to then turn to their own books. In this bend, you'll read aloud a story across two days. You read the first half of the story in Session 1, and then teach a series of minilessons in which you demonstrate with that part of the text. Then, you read the second half of the story in Session 5, which becomes fuel for the rest of the minilessons. You'll also return to this story in some minilessons in Bend II.

I've suggested a story to read aloud, and a few video clips to show as well. If you follow the plan laid out here, you'll begin with a short story, Adam Bagdasarian's "Popularity," from *First French Kiss*. The main character, Will, appears again in the story that launches Bend II, "The Fight," also from *First French Kiss*. Because we typically don't have the time to read aloud a novel in secondary classes, using two stories from a collection about the same character creates an opportunity to follow a character over time and develop more complex thinking. The minilessons return to the read-aloud text, and also introduce some video clips that give students the chance to work across texts.

All the time, students will practice the reading work in the novels they are reading on their own. Keep an eye on your readers' volume. If kids are finishing a book every four or five days, they are probably fine. If they are taking much longer, consider whether they are well-matched to their books. You'll see that this bend ends with a session that invites students to reflect on how reading is going so far, with particular emphasis on reading volume and on making sure that their writing about reading is becoming more purposeful.

Your students will need Post-its (or some way of annotating) and reading notebooks to hold onto their thinking about their books, and also so they (and you) can study how that thinking is growing. They'll begin the unit doing mostly small jottings, which they can keep first in their books and then move to their notebooks, then they'll develop theory charts, and later they'll use their jots to think and write with more insight. It is important to make sure that these notes become more insightful and more purposeful over time.

You should feel free to vary the texts across this bend. It's somewhat easier to vary the digital texts—the video clips—than it is the short story, as so much of each lesson hinges on particular excerpts of this story, but it can be done, of course. Just look across the upcoming teaching, and match parts of your text to upcoming sessions—and consider how your thinking about the character you are studying will grow across each session. The main thing is to be restrained in your demonstrations, so that you show how your thinking grows across the bend.

Choosing texts is also a way to decrease or increase the complexity of the unit overall. The beautiful thing about character work is that it grows in complexity simply by working with a more complex text, so that a strategy that was interesting in a story by Cynthia Rylant becomes even more interesting in a story by Adam Bagdasarian and even more interesting in a story by Sherman Alexie.

If students are each reading a few books across this unit that are at the outside edge of their zone of proximal development, they should find this character work challenging and fascinating. They may not be expert at it right away. That's okay! In more complicated teen literature, the characters are legitimately confusing, complex, and sometimes frustrating. They merit deep study, like the teen readers you are teaching.

All the best,
Mary Ehrenworth

Letter to Teachers—Day Zero

Dear Teachers,

Before this unit begins, there are a few steps we recommend you take so that on Day One, you can jump right into the work of the unit. These steps include: setting up an engaging and supportive classroom library, assessing your readers and studying their reading data, helping them to choose books they can read with high levels of accuracy, starting them on courses of study in which they will read books within a series or a genre or books written by the same author, and pairing them with a partner at a similar reading level. These steps are detailed below.

To support your planning, you might want to skim a few of the early chapters in *A Guide to the Reading Workshop: Middle School Grades* on classroom libraries, assessment, and matching readers to books. You might read them with a colleague or two, talking over how you'll develop systems in your classroom, grade level, and school so that you and your readers will thrive. I include you and your need to thrive in this equation because it is no small matter to keep track of sixty to a hundred readers, or more, as many middle school teachers do. How much time you get to spend with kids each day, how accessible your data are, how well stocked and appealing your library is—these factors may feel somewhat out of your control, and yet have a profound impact on students' reading success.

ORGANIZING THE CLASSROOM LIBRARY

Your classroom library will be the lifeblood of your reading workshop. The time you take to stock and organize your classroom library before students arrive for the first day of school will prove invaluable. There is help for you in the *A Guide to the Reading Workshop: Middle School Grades* and *A Guide to the Teachers College Reading and Writing Project Classroom Libraries* on organizing your classroom library to support students' reading growth and independence.

The most important thing is that your library be engaging. Baskets of books grouped by series, author, and genre encourage kids to organize their reading lives in similar ways.

MATCHING READERS TO BOOKS

In the first few days of the school year, your work will be to ensure that students have books in hand, so that when you officially begin the unit, you and your students can be off and running. Students have a few options for getting books, and you'll want to encourage them to use all of them. They have the classroom library, which hopefully contains a solid starter set of books to entice readers. They have school and public libraries. They can download e-books to their digital devices. They can buy, trade, or swap books. Inspire your students to make books central to their lives.

Part of the work of getting books into kids' hands includes making sure they are choosing books they can read well, books that are at an appropriate level of difficulty. If your students are reading workshop veterans, expect that they already know a lot about choosing books wisely. If they are sixth-graders, they probably know their reading levels from fifth grade, and will be comfortable looking for books at their levels to start with. You can make it easy for them by having many of your books marked with the level either on the basket or inside the cover, or both. They'll also know the authors and genres they like.

Meanwhile, you'll know something about your readers from their state testing data. Make sure you have these data, and be alert for students who scored below proficient. Chances are, they are reading below grade level. Make sure that these students choose within-reach books that will engage them and avoid choosing too-hard books to lug around like paperweights. As soon as possible, see if you or a learning specialist can do some finer assessment, hopefully a quick running record to get an idea what level books these readers need. For now, recommend books that students think they can "read fast and furiously," finishing them in about four to five days. This suggestion often helps middle school kids feel comfortable choosing appropriate books. Talk up some lower-level books so that kids want to read them. Encourage students who tested as proficient or who you surmise are reading on grade level to think about authors and genres they love, and to choose books they think will help them get back into reading if they didn't read a lot over the summer.

ORGANIZING PARTNERSHIPS

Before the unit officially begins, we also recommend you match students up with a partner. Ideally, partners will be at similar reading levels, particularly if you plan on channeling them to read the same books together. If you end up with one or two partnerships that are not at similar levels, see if they might enjoy the same genre for now, and then sort out better partnerships as soon as you can. Across Bend I, as you get to know your students even better, and they get to know themselves as readers, you may help renegotiate some partnerships so that they make more sense and are more productive.

SETTING UP COURSES OF STUDY

Before the unit officially begins, we also recommend you channel students to choose courses of study that they will pursue throughout Bend I. In so doing, you make the work of this unit more sophisticated than what students may have done in earlier years, and, perhaps more importantly, you support volume, as they will have a lineup of engaging books in their queues. Suggest that they think about authors or genres they have loved, or a series they've been dying to read, and choose two to three books they will read one after the other as a course of study. If you have enough partner books for students to read in same-book partnerships, that would be ideal. If not, partners can swap books, or choose a series together, or choose a similar genre.

Fantasy

Droon → Dragon Slayer Academy → How to Train Your Dragon → Spiderwick Chronicles → Deltora Quest → Narnia → Lightning Thief → Rowan of Rin → Fablehaven → Book of Three → Harry Potter → the Last Dragon → Gregor the Overlander → Graceling → Eragon → Inkheart → Maximum Ride → Mortal Instruments* → Monstrumologist → Night Angel Trilogy* → Farseer Trilogy* → Rain Wild Chronicles* → Lord of the Rings

Dystopian

Gone → Warriors → Among the Hidden → Maze Runners → Legend → City of Ember → Forest of Hands and Teeth → Matched → Divergent The Giver → Little Brother → Cinder → Legend → The 5th Wave → Hunger Games → Chaos Walking → Incarceron → Delirium The Uglies* → An Ember in the Ashes → Lunar Chronicles → Unwind → Enders Game → Ray Bradbury stories → George Orwell novels*

An excerpt from Some Courses of Study for Teen Readers

PLANNING YOUR FIRST READING WORKSHOPS

To create urgency, intensity, and engagement, we recommend you guide your students through full reading workshop sessions, even on the first days of school. This means that you will teach minilessons and will give students some time to read independently while you confer. We leave you to make decisions about how many days of teaching you will need to match kids to books, set them on courses of study, and guide them to choose partners. If your students are experienced with reading workshop, you may be able to accomplish all of this in a single day, or two at the most. If your students are new to reading workshop, it may take a few more days to have all the systems in place to launch the unit successfully.

For students experienced with reading workshop, you may want to teach that readers rely on strategies they've learned in school and from their own experiences to choose books wisely (like looking at the length, the covers, the font, reading a little bit). Then give a tip that it makes sense to choose a few books at a time, or at least have them in mind, so that they are on a kind of "course of study." For a class where many students are less experienced readers, you may want to teach that readers often choose books at the start of the year that help them get back into reading, ones that they can read quickly, so they can get to know some authors and genres and see what helps them read more. On another day, you might introduce the idea of courses of study, and teach that a smart course of study might be a series.

Plan for your minilessons to run about ten minutes, then dedicate a few minutes of your workshop time for students to browse, either the shelves or in baskets that you've placed on desks (perhaps strategically using your data). Then watch how kids begin to read. You'll know there's trouble if you see a few students looking up often, not turning pages—signs that they're in a book that is too hard.

In your conferring and small-group work, then, you can address kids who seem to be struggling with their books. They may have read only a few pages, may be already putting a book down, or may not look as if they are reading. You can tackle these kids one-on-one, or in the interest of time, you might talk with one and pull in another reader with a similar issue. Lean on your knowledge of levels, authors, and genres to help them into better matches. Here are some tips you might give kids:

At the end of a minilesson, gather students for a share, in which you suggest ways that they can track their reading volume to help them stay in a solid reading zone. Middle school students (perhaps all students) can find reading logs an exercise in frustration if they become an exercise in obedience. So it's important to offer choice, and manageable and appealing systems. You might say to students, "You'll want to develop a simple system to help you keep track of your reading, so you'll be able to reflect on how it's going." It could be a paper reading log, it could be an app, like You-Log, for a smart phone or tablet, or it could be on a calendar.

> ### Extra Tips for Choosing New Books When You Feel Stuck
> **Think about your <u>reading level</u>.**
>
> Ask yourself: What kinds of books was I reading at the end of last year? What level was I reading easily? Then look for books that look and feel like that, or that are marked with that level. It's smart to start the year with fast-and-furious reading, which means choosing just-right books.
>
> **Think about <u>authors you've loved</u>.**
>
> If you loved Judy Blume, she writes a lot of books at different levels. So do prolific authors such as Suzanne Collins, Matt Christopher, Mike Lupica, Walter Dean Myers, Matt de la Peña, Jacqueline Woodson, and Avi. Look for an author you recognize. Pick up some of his or her books. See if one feels right.
>
> **Think about <u>genres you've enjoyed</u>, in books or movies.**
>
> If you love dystopian, check out series like Divergent, Gone, The Maze Runner. If you love thrillers, check out Alex Rider. If you love sci-fi like Star Trek, check out the Artemis Fowl series. If you love romance and tragedy, find anything by John Green. If you like sports stories, try books by Matt Christopher, Chris Crutcher, Mike Lupica, Matt de la Peña.

You might then say, "All you need is a way that, every week or so, you can look back on how reading has been going, and see how often you've been in a reading zone. Any day, across school and home, when you read somewhere between forty and sixty pages, you are reading in a solid reading zone. That might be twenty pages in school and twenty outside. If you need to start with an easier goal, start with thirty to forty pages. The main thing is, you need a way to look back, over time, and see how many books you've read, what kinds of books they've been, and how often you've been in the reading zone. That information will help you reflect, choose books, and achieve your goals." Share examples of different systems, and have students choose a system to pilot for the rest of this week.

These are lofty goals for the launch of this unit: to get kids into books, to do your best to make sure they are in books they can read, and to help them start preliminary systems for keeping track of reading. Kids won't be perfect at any of this, and they won't all be the same. At the start of the year, some kids find books easily. Some come with books and tell you what *you* should be reading. Some act as if they've never had to choose a book in

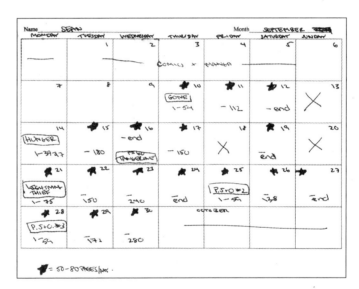

FIG. O–1 Students set up different systems to track their own reading.

their life and you have put them up in front of a firing squad. Have faith. There is a book for every reader; you just have to have patience, belief, and the willingness to seek out books for every child.

All the best,
Mary Ehrenworth

Session 1

Read-Aloud

Investigating Multiple Character Traits

GETTING READY

- Prior to today's session, you will need to study your assessment data, channel students toward independent reading books that they can read with high comprehension, and help each get onto a course of study (e.g., historical fiction or a series), which they may share with a partner who will be reading the same books or similar books. See "Letter to Teachers—Day Zero" for more details.

- Choose your read-aloud (here it is "Popularity" by Adam Bagdasarian, from *First French Kiss*). Prepare your read-aloud by noting places in the text where you will demonstrate a strategy or prompt students to practice that strategy. Anticipate the coaching or feedback you'll give to students as they try the work.

- Convene students for the read-aloud, each sitting beside his or her partner and each with a few Post-its and a reading notebook they can place these in. For now, expect that some students may jot during the read-aloud and others won't, but they will all jot a Post-it or two during reading time (see Link and Conducting the Read-Aloud).

- In instances when students anticipate the work you would otherwise be coaching toward, prepare to give feedback that celebrates what they are already doing (see Conducting the Read-Aloud).

- Prepare to record students' thinking on oversized Post-its you display on chart paper titled, "Will's Character Traits in 'Popularity'" (see Conducting the Read-Aloud).

- Display Bend I anchor chart, "To Think Deeply about Characters" (see Conducting the Read-Aloud).

- Be prepared to give some comments as you "lean-in" while students read independently (see Independent Reading).

IN THIS SESSION

TODAY YOU'LL read aloud the first half of "Popularity" by Adam Bagdasarian, from *First French Kiss*. You will teach students that subtle details can give a lot of information about a character, especially about their traits.

TODAY YOUR STUDENTS will spend most of the session participating in the read-aloud, and then spend a brief time reading a book they chose earlier. As they read, they'll identify character traits and capture their thinking on Post-its. Their Post-its will make visible the work they are doing musing over the best word to use for a specific trait.

CONNECTION

Introduce the work of read-aloud. Explain that you'll read aloud in such a way that you introduce new reading work, first demonstrating, then coaching as kids try it.

"Readers, today we dive into the work of turning you into ever-more powerful and expert readers. Here's how our reading work will go this year.

"For each unit, there will bends in the unit, like the mountain trail switchbacks that bikers and hikers use. Experienced climbers go up gradually, climbing diagonally in one direction, and then make a switchback into another direction. The bends in the path help them travel through harder and harder terrain. In the same way, you'll have bends in each unit of study, and each bend will put you on harder reading terrain.

"In this unit, you'll do the thinking work that all readers of novels do—a deep study of characters. This work is the heart of all reading work. Chances are, you've done some character work before, so you'll work on making your reading work more complex and sophisticated, like the novels that you're reading.

"Today, and most of the time, we'll begin each bend in our units of study with a read-aloud, and that text will be woven through later minilessons. Today, and during every read-aloud, I'll launch some new thinking work, demonstrate it, and then you'll try that work by talking with your partner.

"I'll listen in and coach from the sidelines, giving you feedback. Then you'll have a chance to transfer that same thinking to your own books."

Channel kids to orient themselves to the text and then to listen, attentive to details to discern character traits. Set them up to learn from the way you do the work.

"Today, we'll read and think about a short story by Adam Bagdasarian. It's a short story from a collection called *First French Kiss and Other Traumas*. If you skimmed this collection, you'd find out that the narrator in all the stories, the character who is telling the story, is named Will, and that in each story he's a slightly different age. In this story, Will is in fourth grade. It's called 'Popularity.'

"Readers, whenever you start a story, you want to plan your thinking work. Beginnings of stories, and especially beginnings of short stories, come at you quickly, so it helps to get ready by asking yourself, 'What sort of thinking will I be doing?' Think about what you imagine us doing at the start of this text."

After a moment, I said, "You'll never go wrong if you approach a story thinking about the people, the characters. Begin studying clues about characters' traits early in the story, paying close attention to small details. In the stories you're reading now, even the smallest detail about a character can give you insight.

"As I read, try to do this work, paying close attention to small details so you develop ideas about characters' traits. I'll do some thinking work aloud. Listen as I do this. Compare your thinking with mine."

Though this is a read-aloud, not a minilesson, we start with a connection. The principle that learners do better when they can connect new learning to what they already know holds true in read-aloud sessions as well.

When you explain how your reading work will go this year, you usher students into the community of your classroom. When students can predict how the work will go, they are freed up from trying to figure out the norms of the class and will have more energy to take on grander thinking work right away. If your students come from a reading workshop background, much of this explanation will be familiar to them.

Providing a brief text introduction like this can be especially supportive for English language learners and readers who read below benchmark.

CONDUCTING THE READ-ALOUD

Read aloud the first excerpt of the story without pausing.

Popularity

Somewhere inside me I knew that ten-year-old boys were not supposed to spend their recess circling oak trees in search of four-leaf clovers. Still, that's what I and my equally unpopular acquaintances, Allan Gold and Allan Shipman, were doing while the rest of our classmates played tag and kickball and pushed each other higher and higher on the swings.

Aside from having a little more than our share of baby fat, the two Allans and I had very little in common. In fact, we could barely stand one another. Still, during recess we were the only company we had, so we tried to make the best of it. Now and then one of us would bend forward, pick a clover, examine it, shake his head, and let it fall to the ground.

"Got one," Allan Gold said.

"Let's see," Allan Shipman said.

Allan showed Allan the clover.

"That's only three."

"No, that's four. Right here. See?"

"That's not a whole leaf," Allan Shipman said sourly. "There's one leaf, two leafs, three leafs."

"Four leafs!"

"That's not a whole leaf!"

We had been looking for four-leaf clovers every school day for six months. And each of us knew exactly what he would do if he ever found one: he would hold the lucky clover tight in his hand, close his eyes, and wish he was so popular that he would never have to spend time with the other two again.

Demonstrate how you consider the character's dominant traits. Show a willingness to ponder, exaggerating how you are thinking back over the story and weighing preliminary ideas.

"Let's work on Will's character traits. Think alongside me. Hmm, . . . I think one trait that emerges is that he's *bitter* about hunting for clovers, don't you think? Let me think about evidence for that." I reread a bit muttering, "Will said, um, what was it . . ." Referencing the text, I reread, in a snarky, unhappy voice:

> My equally unpopular acquaintances . . . during recess we were the only company we had . . . for six months!

"It doesn't sound like Will has accepted being with the Allans. The way he talks about them, and this clover picking . . . it sounds *bitter*. Hmm, . . . Is it bitter, or *sarcastic*? I'm not sure. I'll write both terms." I jotted on one oversized Post-it:

> Bitter—or sarcastic?

There is a big difference between "Watch me while I think about . . ." and "Think alongside me." When you can, invite students to take an active role in the lesson, even if you simply ask them to think with you while you demonstrate a strategy.

Step out of the role of reader to explain that you *could* stop your teaching there, but instead, you and your readers can push yourselves to do even more thinking, aware that characters are complex.

"We could stop there. The work I did is work you need to do as you read, and especially the work you need to do as you start new books. You'll definitely want to think about the traits of the characters in your books—and to do as I did, thinking carefully about the precise word for whatever it is you are thinking.

"But here's the thing. Will might be bitter, he might be sarcastic—but he's also other things. In the kinds of books you're reading, characters are complicated. Even in this first scene, we should consider if there are other possible character traits for Will. What else were you thinking about Will? Any thoughts of other traits? Turn and talk to your partner."

Listen in and coach students to provide evidence for their ideas and to use specific, literary words for traits. Coach so that other students can overhear and benefit, so they become stronger partners.

In one partnership, a student explained that Will seemed *lonely*. I said to her partner, "Do you agree? Talk back to each other's ideas, and give evidence for your points. Nudge each other to consider more than one possible term for a character trait."

Another student said that Will seemed *mean* in how he planned to abandon the Allans. I whispered to her partner, "Coach her to consider other possible words to use. There are twenty shades of mean. Ask her to clarify whether he is just a little mean—uncaring, or more mean—unkind. Or is he ruthless?"

Debrief, naming the work you did as a series of replicable transferable steps. Readers notice how small details suggest larger character traits.

"Readers, I heard you use some other words to describe some of Will's possible character traits. One partnership was talking about whether Will is *lonely*, or is the best word *isolated*?" I jotted those two terms on a second enlarged Post-it. "Is he *uncaring* or *ruthless*?"

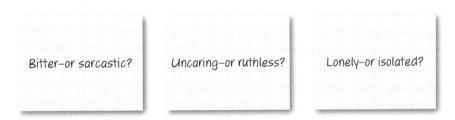

"What's great about the work you just did is that you thought about small details in the story, and how those are suggestive of Will's possible traits. The story never actually says, 'and so this shows that Will was a sarcastic

Help students to lift the level of their partnership work right from the start. Keep your comments transferable. That is, give the kind of feedback that would benefit a partnership on another day, and speak so that other partnerships can overhear your feedback and benefit.

and lonely boy . . .' You did that thinking, instead. And you worked to find the precisely right term for character traits that aren't easily captured by one word."

Read on, inviting students to continue this work, analyzing character traits.

"Are you ready to gather more evidence for traits you have in mind, and to discern new ones if they arise? Maybe you can begin to weigh which traits seem strongest—because there's the most evidence for them.

"You'll have to decide if you want to jot as you listen, or hold details in your head. Some readers love to jot to hold onto details. Others lose the story if they are writing. You decide.

"The main thing is to be thinking hard about what Will says, what he does, and what he thinks, and what these details reveal about him." Then I read aloud from the text:

"Got one!" Allan Shipman said.

Allan Gold swiped the clover from him. "One, two, three," he said, throwing it to the ground.

"There's four there! That was a four-leaf clover! Pick it up!"

"You pick it up!"

"You pick it up!"

"You!"

"You!"

While the two Allans faced off, I looked across the black tar and asphalt at a crowd of boys who were making more noise and seemed to be having more fun than anyone else on the playground. These were the popular boys, and in the center of this group stood their leader, Sean Owens.

Sean Owens was the best student in the fourth grade. He was also one of the humblest, handsomest, strongest, fastest, most clear-thinking ten-year-olds that God ever placed on the face of the earth. Sean Owens could run the fifty-yard dash in six seconds, hit a baseball two hundred feet, and throw a football forty yards. The only thing Sean didn't have was a personality. He didn't need one. When you can hit a baseball two hundred feet, all you have to do is round the bases and wait for the world's adulation.

I gazed at Sean and the rest of the popular boys in bewildered admiration. It seemed like only yesterday that we had all played kickball, dodgeball, and basketball together; and then one morning I awoke to find that this happy democracy had devolved into a monarchy of kings and queens, dukes and duchesses, lords and ladies. It did not take a genius to know that, upon the continent of this playground, the two Allans and I were stableboys.

I had been resigned to my rank for many months, but now, looking at the two Allans (still arguing over the same three-leaf clover), then at the popular boys, I suddenly knew that I could not stand another day at the bottom. I wanted to be a part of the noise and the laughter; I wanted, I *needed*, to be popular.

Prompt partners to compare their thinking about traits, and their evidence for their ideas.

"Readers, before you talk, get your best thinking about character traits ready, not just your first thinking." I gave students a moment to gather their thoughts. "Go ahead, compare with a partner. What traits do you see as being strongest so far? What's your evidence?"

As partners talked, I coached different readers to push their discussions in two directions—from traits to evidence—and from details to how details suggest a trait.

One student was explaining to her partner that Will's strongest character trait so far is his bitterness. I said, "Do you have evidence that Will is bitter? What makes you say that?"

I listened in to another partnership discussing the way Will speaks. I said, "Hmm, . . . you seem to be talking about the words Will used about duchesses and courts . . . so what word would you use to describe him?"

Summarize to help all students, and then give them short, focused feedback to lift the level of their talk in partnerships, often in the form of a tip.

"Readers, let me gather you back. I heard some of you say that the way Will talks about Sean *is* bitter and I love the way you are reading on, holding your initial ideas in mind and collecting more evidence around those ideas. I also like that you thought about many sides of Will. I heard one of you say that Will seems *clever*, the way he talks about kids in the playground being like kings and queens and duchesses and stable boys. When you think you've found a word, ask yourself if it is the precisely right one. Is he clever or observant? Or both? Either way, I'm glad you see that sometimes a new scene helps us gather new ideas.

"Here's a tip to help you raise the level of your thinking and talking. Sometimes when your partner says something smart, something you agree with, here's what you're doing." I mimed nodding.

"My suggestion is do less nodding and more, 'What in the text makes you say that?!' Ask your partner to show you the relevant details in the story. Demand evidence, readers!"

Ready readers to go on, reminding them to raise the level of their work by supporting their ideas with specific text evidence.

"Right, readers, let's read on, and be ready to talk about your ideas . . . and your evidence."

Being ten years old, I did not question this ambition, but I did wonder how on earth I was going to realize it. Though I only stood twenty yards from the heart of the kingdom, I felt a thousand miles removed from the rank and prestige of its citizens. How could I bridge such a gap, knowing I might be stared at, or laughed at, or belittled to a speck so small that I could no longer be seen by the naked eye? And as I stood on that playground, torn between fear and ambition, those twenty yards began to recede from view, and I knew that I must either step forward now, or retreat forever to a life of bitter companions and three-leaf clovers.

I took a deep breath and then, with great trepidation, crossed the twenty longest yards I had ever walked in my life and found myself standing a few feet from the outer circle of what I hoped was my destiny. I lowered my head a little, so as not to draw attention to myself, and watched and listened.

Mitch Brockman, a lean, long-faced comic, considered by many to be the funniest boy in the fourth grade, was in the middle of a story that had something to do with Tijuana

> and a wiener mobile. I wasn't sure what the story was about, but there was a lot of body English and innuendo, all of which the crowd seemed to find absolutely hilarious.
>
> I noticed that every time Mitch said something funny, he eyed Sean Owens to see if he was laughing. He was. Silently. His mouth was open, but it was the laughter of the other boys that filled the silence. I realized then that Mitch was Sean's jester. As long as he could make Sean laugh, he was assured a prominent position in the group.
>
> I wondered what *my* position in the group might be. I certainly wasn't a great athlete, student, or ladies' man, but I did have a sense of humor. Maybe I could be the *second-funniest* boy in the fourth grade. My thoughts went no further because the bell ending recess rang. But that night, just before I fell asleep, I saw myself standing in the center of the popular boys telling the funniest stories anyone had ever heard. I saw Sean Owens doubled up with laughter. I saw myself triumphant.
>
> I returned to the group every recess, for three days. I stood, unnoticed, just outside the outer circle, waiting for my moment, for the one joke or wisecrack that would make me popular. I knew that I would only get one chance to prove myself, and that if I failed, I would be sent back to the stables. And so, with the single-mindedness of a scientist, I listened to the jokes the other boys made, hoping to align my comic sensibilities with theirs. Now and then I found myself on the verge of saying something, but every time I opened my mouth to speak, Mitch would launch into another routine, and my moment passed, and I had to resign myself to yet another day in the dark.
>
> I did not know then that popularity has a life span, and that Mitch's time was about to run out.

First, retell the part of the story to support students' thinking about new traits. Then, invite them to compare their thinking with partners.

"Readers, this part is interesting, right? It feels like we're seeing a new side of Will here—how he watches for days, studying Mitch, Owen, and the boys like a scientist . . . fascinating! What do you think? Do you see any new traits emerging? What words would you use for those traits? Think for a second to prepare for your conversation with your partner. What words would you use to describe Will? What details support your thinking?" I waited for a moment, then said: "Now compare with your partner!"

Listen in, and give some feedback that strengthens partner talk.

I turned to one partner and said, "Your partner said Will seems determined here . . . remember, don't just nod. Go ahead and ask, 'What makes you say that?'"

To another student I said, "You're saying that Will seems *observant*. I bet that's a word you've been using in science. It's true, it feels like he's watching these kids like they are a science experiment. Fascinating! It's great that you're using such a specific word for his trait. Find out if your partner agrees."

I overheard another student describing Will as *fake*. To her partner I said, "Find out what she means by that, that she thinks Will is fake. Demand evidence!"

Record and share students' observations.

"Readers, here are some traits you're naming." I gestured to the chart on which I'd collected some of their overheard conversations. "We'll keep these initial traits in mind as we continue to learn about Will."

As partners talk, you can help them use more literary language. So, if a student says that Will seems to know that popularity is fleeting, you might suggest, "Oh, so you think he's conflicted?" As in, he wants to be popular even though he knows it won't last?" Often, kids have sophisticated ideas, but don't have the vocabulary to express them.

Will's Character Traits in "Popularity"

- Bitter—or sarcastic?
- Clever—or observant?
- Uncaring—or ruthless?
- Determined—or??

Reveal the anchor chart for this bend, then wrap up with a recap of students' reading work and partnership work.

"Let's summarize the work you've done so far today." I revealed our anchor chart and read aloud the bullet point.

ANCHOR CHART

To Think Deeply about Characters . . .

- **Expect characters to be complicated and show more than one trait.**

"In your work as readers, you're doing three significant things. First, you're not satisfied with your first thinking and first trait. Instead, you keep thinking and theorizing, asking yourself, 'What new traits are emerging here?' Second, you're considering your partner's ideas as well, and realizing that readers see different things in the same story. That's the beauty of collective interpretation. And third, you are demanding evidence. No more nodding. Instead I'm hearing, 'What in the text makes you say that?!'"

LINK

Channel students to read independently, trying this work in their own books.

"You have about ten minutes to try this work in your own books. As you read, collect a Post-it or two about characters that interest you in your book. Maybe read for a few minutes and pause to jot—or you might reread a bit, jot a Post-it, and then read on. Either way, I recommend your jots be in the form of questions, as we did with 'Bitter—or sarcastic?' Try to think of more than one side to a character.

"But mostly, *read!* It should look like books in hands, you bent over them, and a quiet room."

Just as we do in minilessons, we end read-aloud sessions with a link. We tuck new learning into students' repertoires, and we give them a tip or two to fuel their independent reading time.

SESSION 1: READ-ALOUD

INDEPENDENT READING

Getting the Work of the Unit Up and Running with Lots of Energy

Soon, you'll plan deliberate reading conferences, working with one student or pulling together three or four students for strategic small-group work. Right now, though, you don't have much time because the read-aloud will have been much longer than a usual minilesson. Also, all your students need to feel your attention. That means you'll want to circulate rapidly, getting to as many students as you can.

Although you will have already helped channel kids to books they can read, be sure that you continue to keep an eye on that now. Remember that at the start of the year, it helps for kids to choose what they'll refer to as an "easy book." You will want them moving through books rapidly. It's not going to help a reader who reads at levels R–S to carry around Harry Potter, Book 7, for eight weeks like a giant paperweight. You might note the books kids have chosen, remarking on their choices, giving help if any kid seems to have chosen poorly. The rule of thumb is that kids should be able to read about ¾ of a page a minute, so if you see a student who is still on page 1 after five minutes of reading, that should sound alarms.

You'll also want to stir up enthusiasm for students' early character work. Look for signs that readers are approximating the work you've taught, like a Post-it note with words that capture a character's possible traits.

As you circulate, keep in mind that your goal is to make the kids feel visible, and to stir up enthusiasm for reading and for the new character work. Some comments that might help with this work follow.

"Lean-in" Comments about Book Choices

- I love that book! I can't wait to hear what you think about it!
- I love that author! Let me know how that book is. I haven't yet read it.
- That book has a lot of people talking about it. You'll have to let us know what you think.
- There's a movie based on that book, isn't there? It will be interesting to see how they compare.
- Is that book part of a series? Is it the first one?
- I wanted to read that, but it looked a little hard. Tell me how it goes.
- Oh, I'd like to read that too. Maybe we could make a little book club on it.

> **"Lean-in" Comments about Early Character Work**
> - You already noticed one trait your character displayed! What's your best evidence?
> - Wow! Your character must be incredibly complicated. You've already found three character traits!
> - Two traits! I bet you're already thinking about which trait is stronger, right?
> - Oh, that's interesting. I wonder if that will turn out to be more of an emotion in this scene, or a trait across the story.

SHARE

Ask readers to share which character they find most intriguing in their novels—and then prepare to continue this thinking as they read tonight.

"You're all deep into reading, so we just have a moment for a share. Briefly, tell your partner about the character you are finding most interesting in your novel so far, and share some of your early thoughts about the character. You might draw on one of your Post-its as you talk.

"Then put a couple of blank Post-its in your book, stuck inside the cover, so tonight, as you read on, you'll be ready to note where you find signs of interesting character traits."

SESSION 1 HOMEWORK

KEEP TRACK OF HOW MUCH YOU READ—AND JOT NOTES ON CHARACTER TRAITS

Tonight, get lots of reading done. Plan to read for *at least* thirty minutes (keep going if you're loving your book). For tonight, would you also capture how many pages you read in thirty minutes? That will help you with goal-setting later. Then, of course, keep reading if you're in a reading zone. Keep track of where you start tonight and the page on which you end, and the number of minutes you read.

As you read, notice when you are learning about character traits and make sure you continue to jot the most interesting traits on Post-its. Tuck these into your book or into your reading notebook.

Session 2

Readers Revise Their Thinking as They Accumulate Evidence

GETTING READY

- Display and add to chart, "Will's Character Traits in 'Popularity'" (see Connection and Teaching).
- Ask students to bring their books and reading notebooks with the Post-it notes they jotted last night to the minilesson (see Connection and Active Engagement).
- Display "A Theory Chart" (see Teaching).
- Display the part of the read-aloud text you read yesterday (see Teaching).
- Display and add to anchor chart, "To Think Deeply about Characters" (see Link).
- Distribute large Post-it notes to each student that they can use to create their theory charts (see Link).
- Create and show examples of word charts. Provide paint chips or colored slips of paper for kids to make their own word charts. You may also want to provide baggies with cutout words that go together for kids to sort (see Conferring and Small-Group Work).
- Ask students to bring their reading notebooks to the meeting area (see Share).
- Be prepared to show the "Optional Ideas for Your Reader's Notebook" chart, and sample notebook pages (see Share and Homework).

IN THIS SESSION

TODAY YOU'LL teach that characters reveal themselves over time, and that readers must remain alert to new details and be willing to rethink their initial ideas. You'll demonstrate this in the read-aloud text, showing kids how you can make a theory chart that shows evidence of (and revision of) your theories.

TODAY YOUR STUDENTS will read on in their books with their theories of characters in mind. As they read, they'll reevaluate and revise their thinking about characters' traits, supporting that new thinking with text evidence. They will add this evidence to the previous day's Post-its to create theory charts. They will also begin the serious work of keeping a reader's notebook.

MINILESSON

CONNECTION

Invite students to consider the thinking work they did the night before in their own books, and to share one insight with a partner.

"Readers, yesterday we did some important reading work in 'Popularity.'" I motioned to our chart of character traits.

Will's Character Traits in "Popularity"

- Bitter–or sarcastic?
- Clever–or observant?
- Uncaring–or ruthless?
- Determined–or??

"Last night, you read your own novels and investigated some of your main character's traits. Now take a second, get out last night's jotting, and put a star on the jot that describes your character's strongest trait or traits."

"Okay, go ahead, which traits seemed especially dominant?" I let them share for a moment.

Listen to students, adding in small comments to add to engagement and strengthen partner talk.

I listened in and offered comments to encourage their thinking and their talk. "Oh, you said that so far, Katniss seems brave. She does seem unusually brave. Do you think she's braver than others in her world?

"You're talking about the older brother in *Tangerine*? He's so intimidating. Your partner hasn't read that book. Can you show him a passage that captures how intimidating he is? See if he agrees if that trait is mean, or if it is something a little different."

Gather students' attention and summarize.

"Readers, let's come back together. The work you did is the same as the work we did in 'Popularity,' but your books are different, so you found different traits. Some characters seem foolish, some seem tough, some seem frankly scary.

"What's most important is that the work you did yesterday isn't work you only do in 'Popularity.' You're doing similar thinking work in your independent books, watching how that thinking plays out differently with the characters in different books.

"As you did this work, did you sometimes find yourself changing your mind as you kept reading? Last night I was rereading *The Hunger Games* and found myself changing my mind about Katniss's traits. At first I thought, 'She's strong.' Then I thought, 'I'm not sure she is that strong and maybe that's why she doesn't trust anyone.' This kind of thinking and rethinking is significant—it's often where your best thinking will occur."

❖ **Name the teaching point.**

"Readers, today I want to teach you that in complicated stories, characters reveal themselves over time. Experienced readers, therefore, are alert to new details, and they are ready to rethink and revise their first ideas in the face of new evidence."

Channeling students to share their homework makes homework meaningful to students and gives you a minute to quickly see who is doing homework and who needs support.

Notice than even when talking with students about specific books, we nudge them to lift the level of their work in transferrable ways. Here, we remind a student to provide evidence from the text, and we show him how to invite his partner into the conversation, even though his partner hasn't read the book.

TEACHING

Demonstrate that readers generate an idea about a character and then read with that idea in mind, looking for evidence to confirm or revise the idea.

"Readers, let's try this work with Will's traits in 'Popularity.'" I displayed the first page of the story and the Post-its we'd made the previous day, documenting Will's character traits. "First, we have an idea about a character. So let's go back to that idea from yesterday, at the start of the story." I turned back to the start of the text, and remembered, "Ah yes, we said that Will seems *bitter*.

"Once you have a theory about a character, it is important to read on with that theory in mind, looking to see if there is compelling evidence to support that theory. Let's look for evidence that Will seems bitter."

Show how you weigh and evaluate evidence to test the strength of that evidence and therefore, of the theory.

"So . . . one piece of evidence that seems strong is that Will talks about how much he hates picking clovers with the Allans. Another is that he has been doing this for six months." I pointed to these parts of the story in the text. Then I added each piece of evidence written onto the Post-it on the chart (bitter—or sarcastic?). By doing this, I created what I refer to as a theory chart.

A Theory Chart

Bitter—or sarcastic?
- Hates picking clover with the Allans
- Has been doing it for six months

Next, make a show of realizing that your thinking about a character is beginning to change, returning to a part from the read-aloud text.

I looked at the chart and the story, pausing to show I was thinking. I ran my finger down a later part of the story. "Hmm, . . . after Will leaves the Allans and joins the popular kids, it's not clear to me whether he is *still* bitter. I'm thinking about whether he was bitter, or was it something else? Or does his personality change?"

There is no need for this chart to be beautifully executed. You are demonstrating a powerful way to use quick jotting to grow ideas about a character. Students need to see that writing about reading can be pointed and brief, and done in service of growing ideas. You will be surprised, though, how much kids like using large or beautiful color Post-its. They are tired of the standard yellow ones. But introduce larger ones, or tiny ones, and they suddenly want to use them.

I read:

> *I wondered what my position in the group might be. I certainly wasn't a great athlete, student, or ladies' man, but I did have a sense of humor. Maybe I could be the second-funniest boy in the fourth grade. My thoughts went no further because the bell ending recess rang. But that night, just before I fell asleep, I saw myself standing in the center of the popular boys telling the funniest stories anyone had ever heard. I saw Sean Owens doubled up with laughter. I saw myself triumphant.*

"Readers, what I'm doing here, that you can also do, is I take a trait and think about whether it really holds true across the text. In this instance, I was kind of expecting Will to go on being bitter forever. But later, as we read on, doesn't he seem kind of different? I'm thinking that he changes across the story.

"Have you ever met someone, formed an opinion about that person, and then as time goes on, you realize he or she is not exactly as you thought originally? Characters in books can be that way too, and it is really important that you look across the book, gathering more and more evidence, and that you realize that evidence will often change your theory about the character.

"Now I'm seeing a new side of Will. Later in the story, he imagines the new position he wants in the group with great detail. He seems hopeful and confident that he can get what he wants. This makes me think he is more optimistic than I realized before. Maybe at the start, he wasn't bitter so much as longing."

A Theory Chart

Bitter ~~or sarcastic?~~ longing?
- Hates picking clover with the Allans
- Has been doing it for six months

→

Then . . . hopeful
- Hopes he can be 2nd funniest in grade
- Imagines new roles he'll play in group

Summarize your work of collecting evidence of a trait, and weighing and evaluating your thinking in the face of new evidence.

"Readers, see what we did? We read on, alert to text that might add to or change our thinking, and as we did, we collected more evidence of the character's traits. We weighed that evidence and rethought our initial theories. We found a way to capture that new thinking on what we call 'A Theory Chart.'"

ACTIVE ENGAGEMENT

Invite students to try out the work in their own stories and to share their thinking with a partner.

"Now it's your turn. I'm sure there are character traits you thought about at the beginning of your stories. Will you focus on one trait now and think about new parts of the story? Do those parts contain more evidence of that trait, or is there evidence that pushes you to revise your thinking? For example, at first I thought Katniss was not just tough, but hard, but then I saw how devastated she was about Rue dying. That doesn't really go with my theory of her being hard. So now, I'm thinking it's not so much that she's *hard* as that she's *determined*.

"What about your novel? Are you far enough in your book to have formed a theory about a character and to have found more evidence that can inform that theory? If you're not that far in your book, think of another book you read, or even a movie you saw. Can you remember a time when you started with one theory about a character, but then when you looked further into the text for more evidence, you ended up thinking new thoughts? When you have an example of a trait you've rethought, give a nod."

I waited for a moment. "Now turn and share with your partner."

I circulated while partners talked, coaching in and gathering their examples. To one student, I said, "You're just starting a book. Do you want to talk about the character in the last book you read, or do you want to talk about Will, about other traits we should rethink?"

To another partnership I offered, "You're reading *The Hunger Games*. So you're saying that Peeta seems weak at first, but actually he's strong? What particular chapter or part got you to think that?"

To a student telling his partner about *Diary of a Wimpy Kid*, I said, "Oh, you're thinking about Greg. You thought he was so thoughtless at first, but now you're thinking he's more than that?"

Reconvene your readers and summarize.

"Readers, you did some nice work. I saw some of you going back to specific pages where you left Post-it notes in your books, and then I saw you looking forward in the text, thinking whether those pages pushed you to change your initial thinking. I saw others of you grouping some of your Post-its in your notebook, under certain traits. If you had more time, you could capture not only your first theory but also your newest thinking on a theory chart, on a large Post-it or in your notebook. You may want to do that later."

Keep in mind that the active engagement portion of your minilesson is a chance for you to gather assessment data. Make a note of students, for instance, who continue to use simple vocabulary to describe their characters, such as mean *or* scared. *You can gather these students later and help them develop more literary vocabulary, with word charts for character traits.*

LINK

Engage readers in making a plan for their reading work during workshop and then send them off.

"Readers, as you go off to read today, it's important to make a plan for your work. You won't be 'just reading . . .' Instead, I know you'll go back to some initial theories about your characters, and then you'll look forward in the text, noticing how upcoming text informs or challenges your initial ideas.

"Will you make sure that today, you don't just collect more Post-its about the characters in your book? Be sure you also read on with some of your initial theories in mind. As you read on, collect more evidence that relates to your theory, or make a decision to revise those theories.

"Before you begin reading, take a second to reread your Post-its, to rethink your ideas, and to capture at least one theory about a character. I'll pass out some big Post-it notes you can use to capture and track your theory as you read. You can put these in your notebooks." I gave students thirty seconds of quiet.

"Take a second and tell your partner which character you're going to investigate today, and what theory you're starting with." After a minute for talking, I channeled the students to get started on their reading.

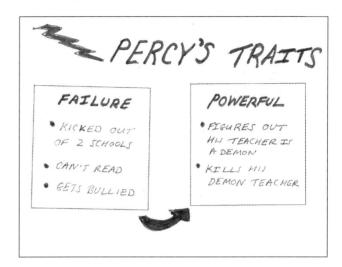

FIG. 2–1 Rethinking Percy Jackson's character traits in theory charts.

 ANCHOR CHART

To Think Deeply about Characters . . .
- Expect characters to be complicated and show more than one trait.
- **Revise your thinking in the face of new evidence.**

I listened for a moment, then sent students off to read, in pairs or singly.

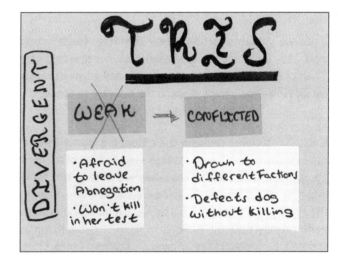

FIG. 2–2 Rethinking Tris' traits in *Divergent*: adding in new text and evidence and rethinking prior evidence.

SESSION 2: READERS REVISE THEIR THINKING AS THEY ACCUMULATE EVIDENCE

CONFERRING AND SMALL-GROUP WORK

Deepening Students' Talk and Writing about Their Characters

TODAY, you'll want to devote a good deal of your time to getting students going on their character work. As you did yesterday, you might spend the first ten minutes or so of the workshop moving around the room, doing quick check-ins with students to celebrate, and at times lift the level of, their character work.

If you see **students who jotted one initial character trait**, and haven't recorded anything else, you could say, "You're getting to know what your character is like as a person. That's *huge* work. I see you jotted one of his character traits. I bet any page now you'll discover even more about your character, maybe another side you hadn't seen before. Have a Post-it ready to record that new trait when you see it."

If you see **students jotting a few character traits**, you might compliment that work, then encourage them to consider which trait is best supported. You might say, "Your character is so complicated. You've noticed your character has a *ton* of different sides. Are you already studying the evidence to see which of these traits is best supported in this book? I can't wait to hear which one becomes her dominant trait."

If you see **students revising their thinking about their character in light of new evidence**, you'll want to make a big deal out of this work. You might pause all the kids at a table, saying, "This reader has already done the work we started today. When he started reading, he had an initial idea about his character's trait, and he thought it was true for sure. But as he read on today, he encountered new evidence that made him revise his earlier thinking. He jotted a Post-it about how his thinking changed. He wrote, 'I used to think . . . but now I think . . .' He also started a trait timeline, and is keeping track of which traits seem to be reinforced across the story, and which begin to drop off or evolve. Very cool."

Doing more extensive work with lifting the level of a student's literary language.

You might notice students describing characters with fairly basic terms. They might jot that Peeta is "nice" or that Malfoy is "mean" or "unkind." If that is the case, you might gather a few students and teach them how to expand their literary vocabulary, so that they use words that more accurately and precisely capture what their characters are like as people.

To start, you might say, "Today I want to teach you that when you're describing your character, look for a word that precisely captures what your character is like." To help students choose more precise character traits, you might introduce them to charts of related words, perhaps written on paint strips, with an easy word in the middle, with the least intense version of the word at the top and the most intense version at the bottom.

You could explain how to use this tool. "I want to describe Katniss in the Arena. I could just say she's scared, but instead I could push myself to figure out if she's *apprehensive*, which is just a little scared, or really scared, like *terrified*."

Then, you might channel students to create additional charts they could use to talk about their characters' traits. You might say, "Now, with someone near you, make one of these charts. I've started some that have words like *happy* or *mean* or *sad* or *proud* or *strong*. There are some baggies containing groups of cutout words that you could sort. I'll come around and help you with words."

As students complete their word charts, channel them to use this information to lift the level of their character trait jots. You might say, "Whenever you're talking about characters, use this language in your conversation and jottings. Try to expand the language you use to describe characters in your novels." Check with these students in the coming days to hold them accountable for incorporating literary language into their jots.

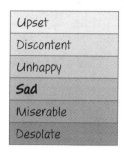

SHARE

Making Reading Notebooks Places Where Readers Work with Choice and Ownership

Rally students to the important and serious work of keeping reading notebooks.

"I don't usually convene you at the end of reading time, but for today, will you join me in the meeting area?" After students gathered, I asked each of them to get out their reading notebooks. "Readers, so far, most of you are using your notebook as a place to keep your Post-its. That's a start, and I love the way some of you are using your Post-its and manipulatives—you are sorting and moving them in your notebook. There is so much more you can do with a reading notebook. Your notebook is a place where you can capture the smartest work you do on your Post-it notes, and it's also a tool where you can grow some really deep thinking."

Introduce a few possibilities for how students can write about their reading. Channel students to plan how they want to write about their reading and to share their plan with their partner.

"This is your notebook, so you'll be the one who ultimately decides what goes on each page. Tonight, you'll focus on creating a notebook page that you want to share with a partner, and it will be up to you how that page goes. Here are a few options." I put up the "Optional Ideas for Your Reader's Notebook" chart and showed a few sample notebook pages.

"Right now, will you plan out the way you'll write about your reading tonight? Once you have a decision, share it with your partner."

Optional Ideas for Your Reader's Notebook

Gather ideas on a few character traits, and choose one that interests you. Then reread and read on, collecting new evidence of that trait. As you do this, let the new evidence change your thinking. You might make theory charts to capture this thinking.

Use a Post-it to capture a trait on a page, then write more off that Post-it. As part of this, you might collect page numbers of pages that support the character trait and jot new thinking you develop as you read on.

Begin to think about traits that a character seems to display on the outside, and ones that are more on the inside, and use small Post-its around a sketch, or in a T-chart, to capture these. Then begin to trace how these traits shift.

Invent other ways to capture and develop your thinking about a character: A sketch? Some questions? A timeline? A T-chart?

SESSION 2 HOMEWORK

READING UP A STORM AND CREATING YOUR FIRST READING NOTEBOOK PAGE

Readers, tonight you have two jobs. First, you should be reading up a storm. Yesterday, you read for at least thirty minutes, and you tracked how many pages you read. Look back at that number. You should be reading *at least* that many pages tonight, and every night from here on out. When you can, go on and read more. Great readers finish the chapter, finish the book, finish the series!

Second, after you read tonight, take a few minutes to create your first reading notebook page, based on the plan you made in school today. You are using your notebook to develop new thinking, so get ready to jot thoughts, to use diagrams, sketches, timelines, and ideas you grow using your Post-its to capture your thinking. Be ready to share your thinking work and notebook pages in class tomorrow.

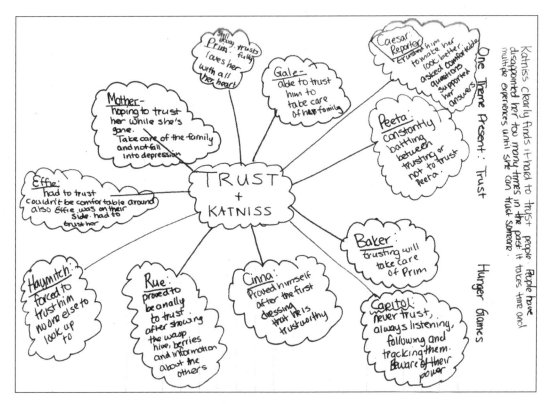

FIG. 2–3 Sample notebook pages can inspire students to love reading notebooks.

Session 3

Developing Courses of Study with a Partner

Book Choices and Thinking Work

Dear Teachers,

In getting ready to launch this unit, your readers chose a few books that they wanted to read, so they could immediately begin to do the work of the unit in these books. These books form a kind of preliminary course of study. Chances are that most of your students chose books within a series or a genre, or perhaps some books by the same author.

Today, you'll suggest that readers also get on a course of study of thinking work. As readers come to know series and genres well, they'll begin to see patterns in the characters—they'll have expectations of the kinds of thinking work around characters that will be interesting. Fantasy readers, for instance, expect to see common fantasy archetypes, just as readers of historical fiction or mystery expect to see archetypes for those genres. As students get to know an author, they'll also recognize similar kinds of characters across that author's novels. All of this means that readers can begin to shape their reading work partly through their knowledge of the kinds of books they are reading.

To begin your minilesson today, you might give students a chance to share the work they did for homework last night in their reading notebooks. To do this, you'll want to give readers a chance to see other readers' notebooks. In your connection, then, you might say something like, "Readers, last night you all graduated from jotting on Post-its to making a page in your reader's notebook. Before doing anything else, let's have a silent share session. For a few minutes, will you exchange your notebook page with someone who's not your partner? After you read that person's notebook page, continue to exchange. Pass your notebooks around a bit. As you look over each other's writing about reading, be thinking, 'What work are some of these readers doing in their notebooks that I might try, too?'"

After kids exchange notebooks for a few minutes, you might gesture for them to reclaim their own notebooks and say something like, "Will you do the most important work of all and read your own reading notebook? Only this time, read it with new eyes. Let all the other notebooks that you have seen fill you with new thoughts about what might be next for you. What can you do to make your reading notebook even more significant?" Let readers talk about this, and suggest that they have goals or ideas in mind for their thinking and writing about reading. Then let them know that you have some thoughts about how they might form some of these goals or ideas, and move to your teaching point.

You'll want to have some books on hand as you make your teaching point, so that you can hold up a fantasy novel, and a historical fiction, and a mystery, and perhaps show a couple of books by Judy Blume or Jacqueline Woodson. Your teaching point might be, "Today I want to remind you that readers take their cues from stories. And different kinds of stories channel readers to do different sorts of thinking work. If you are reading historical fiction, the genre channels you to think in particular ways. If you are reading fantasy, that genre channels you in different ways. It's wise to let the kind of story you are reading influence your plans for thinking about the characters in your novels."

For your teaching and active engagement, you might lead students into a shared inquiry where they quickly think of anything they know about the kinds of characters—and thus character work—that certain genres or authors suggest. You might begin to collect some of this on a chart (which you could have begun earlier and begin to unroll as they talk).

Character Work Some Genres/Authors Suggest

Fantasy	Historical Fiction	Kate DiCamillo
How Characters Fit with or Break with Archetypes unlikely or reluctant hero	*Characters who see injustice and unfairness and want to change things*	*Characters who have suffered losses that shape them*

Your chart will look a little different, as your students may currently be fascinated by different genres, or by certain series. The main thing is not to start a master chart. It's to show that readers are already experts on certain series and genres, and they should use this expertise to guide some of their reading work.

You might finish your lesson with students talking in partners, planning how their genre or author or series knowledge will inform their reading work and how they'll use their Post-its and notebooks to develop some of this reading work. Then send them off to read.

Once students are reading, you might pull some groups based on genre, author, or series and begin to deepen their reading expectations. For this work, you might coauthor, or you might author and share one column of a chart that might begin to have deeper expectations.

Character Work Some Genres/Authors Suggest

Fantasy	Historical Fiction	Mystery	Kate DiCamillo
How Characters Fit with or Break with Archetypes • unlikely or reluctant hero • sidekick relationships • mentor relationship • the character who is not what he or she seems • the complicated villain *Characters who go on journeys or quests*	*Characters who see injustice and unfairness and want to change things* *Characters who display heroism and affect events* *Characters who suffer from historical roles*	*Characters who get misled by false clues and red herrings* *Characters whose flaws interfere with their progress* *Characters whose personal growth turns out to be bigger than solving the mystery*	*Characters who have suffered losses that shape them* *Characters' traits emerge slowly and change across the novel as they grow* *Characters' relationships are complicated and important to the plot*

This may be a good time to review book choices and help students make better choices so they are moving forward as readers. You may want to confer with a student or pull a small group of readers who may want to make fresh choices for their book choices. It may be that the books they chose weren't closely related, or it may be that they could have chosen books that were easier, or more difficult. Often, you can help students stay in the same genre, by considering a kind of ladder of difficulty. In the online resources, you'll find a "courses of study" book list that may be helpful. For example, if a student has chosen the Percy Jackson series, but he is ready to read something more complex, like the Monstrumologist or The Rain Wild Chronicles series, you could recommend that he challenge himself with a new fantasy series. Similarly, if a student is carrying around the Percy Jackson series but your testing data and/or running record data suggest that she reads more at a level O–P, you might entice her into the Spiderwick Chronicles series, which will make a thoughtful course of study for two to three weeks.

For your share, you might want partners to compare with another partnership what they plan to do that night, while they are reading and in their notebooks. Have them explain their choices to each other. Lots of middle school readers who begin to love their reading notebooks will text each other pictures of pages while they are working, and you might suggest that they inspire each other this way, when they are working at night. Then send them off, with homework to read particularly with knowledge of their genre, series, or author in mind, and do more expert reading work that night.

A note for teachers who read this letter over and think, "I don't know if my kids will know anything about genres or authors or series! I don't know if they'll have anything to say during the lesson!" Find out from your kids. Remember, they can think of films (*Titanic*, *The Hunger Games*, *Diary of a Wimpy Kid*) as a way to think about genres. And remember, they'll only talk for a minute, so you're looking for one small bit of their wisdom. And also remember, it's okay to tell them stuff too. You could, for instance, during the small-group work, show some short film clips and help students think through common characteristics of characters in some of these genres. The main thing is not that students are masters at this work. It's that under your influence, they begin to develop and use their growing expertise as readers.

All the best,
Mary

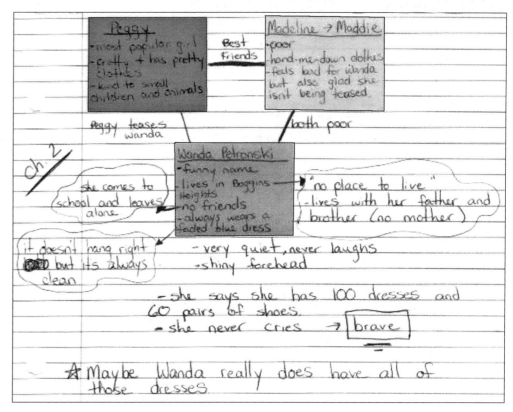

FIG. 3–1 Getting to know multiple characters

SESSION 3: DEVELOPING COURSES OF STUDY WITH A PARTNER

Session 4

Perceptive Readers Acknowledge the Parts of a Character that Are Less Likeable

GETTING READY

✓ Prepare to show a short video clip from *Harry Potter and the Half-Blood Prince*, Sectumsempra scene, starting at the 1:30 mark. A link to the video is available in the online resources (see Active Engagement).

✓ Display and add to anchor chart, "To Think Deeply about Characters" (see Link).

✓ You may want to show literary word charts to some students (see Conferring and Small-Group Work).

✓ Ask students to have their reading notebooks available to discuss entries with partners (see Share).

IN THIS SESSION

TODAY YOU'LL teach students that though it's easy to sympathize with and defend characters, perceptive readers realize that like real people, characters are complex and have less likeable parts.

TODAY YOUR STUDENTS will try noticing parts of characters that are less likeable using a movie clip from a popular film—and then will try this work with characters in their own books. They will continue to explore ways to capture and grow their thinking in their reader's notebooks and will reflect on their strongest examples of writing about reading.

MINILESSON

CONNECTION

Tell a quick story about being unwilling to listen to criticism about a person. Then invite students to share similar experiences.

"Readers, have you ever had the experience of not wanting someone else to criticize a friend or family member? Like I have a brother who can make me crazy, but when someone else criticizes him, I get upset and start defending him. Or, I grew up supporting the Buffalo Bills, who can be a hard football team to support, but if somebody who supports another team criticizes the Bills, I get mad!"

As kids nodded, I invited them to share. "Go ahead, tell your partner—when does this happen to you?"

Reconvene students to debrief, then connect their personal experiences to their character work.

"Readers, let's come back together. I can tell you know exactly what this feels like. When we care about a person, a team, a player, a book, *anything*, it can make us defensive. We can't help it. We find it hard to listen to criticism—which brings me to how we can feel similar emotions about our characters."

❖ **Name the teaching point.**

"Readers, today I want to teach you that it's easy to sympathize with protagonists, or main characters, and want to defend them. Perceptive readers, though, realize that complex characters (like real people) have parts to them that are less likeable."

TEACHING

Demonstrate the way that you, as a reader, carry an awareness that you tend to become biased in favor of a protagonist and therefore have a hard time admitting his or her less likeable parts.

"Let me show you what this looks like. I haven't just been defending my brother, or the Buffalo Bills. I've been defending Will, as well, and sympathizing with his desire to be popular. But maybe I need to look at his behaviors more closely. Now I'm going to close my eyes and think back over parts of the story, with the lens of 'Are there any parts that push me to see other sides of Will, his less likeable sides . . . ?'"

I looked down, as if thinking, and then said, "There was that part at the very beginning, where Will was talking about the Allans. He'd been picking clovers with them for six months, and what does he say? That if he finds a four-leaf clover, the first thing he'd wish was to never spend time with them again."

I looked up and said, "That's kind of repulsive. It's disloyal. But who wouldn't want to be popular? Who wouldn't want to be with the kids playing tag?" Then I paused. "Wait, I think I'm being defensive, protecting Will because he's the main character and I sympathize with him. I have to consider his less likeable sides. The truth is, it's not like he wished they could *all* be popular, or they could *all* escape. He just wants to get away himself. I guess Will can be kind of selfish, if I think about it, and maybe a little mean."

Recap how you pushed yourself to consider the character's less likeable parts.

"Readers, do you see how I caught myself explaining away Will's actions, and realized I was being defensive? Then I pushed myself to consider if some of his actions were not that likeable. It's kind of hard to do, because we want to defend the protagonists in our stories, just like we defend people in our families and friendship groups."

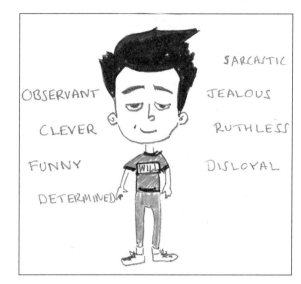

FIG. 4–1   Will's sides

ACTIVE ENGAGEMENT

Set readers up to continue this thinking, using a different popular text for practice.

"Now you try this out. I'll show you a scene from *Harry Potter and the Half-Blood Prince*. You probably remember that for almost all the books and films, Harry is likeable, kind, and compassionate. And there is a student, Malfoy, who teases and bullies Harry. In this scene, Harry catches Malfoy alone in the boy's bathroom. Watch carefully. Do you see any unexpected sides to Harry, possibly less likeable sides?"

I showed the scene, then invited students to talk. "I can tell you have a lot to say. What did you think about how Harry responded when he found Malfoy alone? Tell your partner."

I listened in while partners talked. Then, I reconvened them and summarized what I'd heard. "That was interesting. Some of you discussed how it seems like Malfoy was crying at the sink. I never noticed that. Others talked about how pale and unhappy Malfoy seemed, and yet Harry went right into attacking him. And some of you Harry Potter experts explained that the spell Harry uses, the Sectumsempra, isn't a spell, it's a deadly curse. Which seems pretty extreme. It all makes me want to go read these books again.

"It also reminds me that even good, heroic characters like Harry can have less likeable moments and sides. It's important to push ourselves to consider all the scenes that characters are in and all sides of them, even the less likeable ones."

FIG. 4–2 Harry's sides

LINK

Connect the work readers just practiced to work they can do in their own novels.

"That feeling of being sort of conflicted over a character isn't just about Harry or Will. You may have that feeling sometimes about the main character in your novel. Today, as you go off to read, add this lens to your reading work. Push yourself to see the sides of your characters that may not be the most admirable. I'll add this work to our chart as a reminder, readers.

"Before you get started on your reading and thinking, will you review our anchor chart and think about the reading notebooks you've seen? Set a goal for yourself. What will you do to make your thinking work strong, and to use your reader's notebook work to deepen that thinking?

"You can decide to keep Post-its as you read, and then later to put those Post-its in your notebook. Then again, you could make theory charts about your characters—and read on and on and on, growing ideas about characters. You could take one of those ideas about a character, and think, 'Am I seeing this character through rose-colored glasses?' You can try to see sides of that character that you don't usually see, which might mean you want to make some kind of 'lift the flap' feature, or something. "Whatever you decide to do, decide—and get started."

ANCHOR CHART

To Think Deeply about Characters . . .

- Expect characters to be complicated and show more than one trait.
- Revise your thinking in the face of new evidence.
- **Look at a character's less likeable sides.**

Look at a character's less likeable sides.

CONFERRING AND SMALL-GROUP WORK

Revisiting Traits versus Emotions

TO HELP STUDENTS PROGRESS in their abilities to think about characters, it is important to keep in mind what more developed work looks like. If you pause to think about that, you'll probably quickly come to agree that as readers become more mature, they move from thinking about a character's feelings toward thinking about a character's traits. That is, whereas more novice readers tend to read with blinders on, attending to the current page and to the character's current action, more experienced readers take into account more of the text. More experienced readers think not only about what a character might be feeling at any one point, but about patterns of behavior that span time.

When conferring and leading small groups, you can coach readers to move from thinking about what a character feels at a particular moment toward thinking about that character's ongoing traits. It will help you to keep in mind that texts written at different levels of text complexity support different sorts of character trait work.

Readers who are working with texts at levels K–L–M, for example, will find that in novels at those levels, characters don't necessarily make lots of changes. In The Magic Tree House series, for example, Annie might be momentarily scared in any novel, but the overall pattern quickly emerges that she is brave to the point of recklessness. You can find the pattern again and again.

Once readers progress to books that are a bit more challenging, the work they are asked to do changes. For example, when they read from the Dragon Slayers' Academy series, level N, readers will find they need to read many more pages before they notice breaks in patterns. Therefore thinking about character traits becomes challenging again. And in even more challenging texts such as *Freak the Mighty* or *The Golden Compass*, the patterns emerge more slowly and are harder to see. The texts, then, make challenges that were easy earlier in accessible texts now become challenging.

You'll find, therefore, that you can think about levels of complexity as you coach students to be aware of the difference between traits and emotions. You might tell them that emotions are feelings that are usually fleeting—they don't last long. Emotions are often a response to something that happens. For example, if a character's best friend reveals one of his secrets, the character might feel hurt. But he won't feel that way if he and his friend talk and work things out. Traits, on the other hand, are a more permanent part of a character's personality. You could say a character is sensitive if he often feels hurt by others. You might explain that in more complex texts, it can be more difficult to tell the difference between the two, because characters hold onto emotions for longer stretches of time.

Support higher-level readers in tracking traits and emotions over time.

If you have readers who are working with texts at levels X, Y, and Z (books such as *The Golden Compass*), you may want to convene those readers into a small group and help them with the special challenges they'll encounter. You might say to these readers, "I've been thinking about you as readers, because I notice that in the long books you are reading, the characters are pretty tricky to figure out. In books like the ones you are reading now, characters take a while to reveal themselves, and they can be changeable—they're not the same across the story. So one way readers really get to know these characters is to track their emotions and traits over time."

Tell the group, "It can be interesting to trace characters' emotions, and then study if there are any patterns, or if their emotions are changeable. You might jot some Post-its across the story, and then sort them to try to identify patterns. Or you might note a character's dominant trait in each chapter and see if that trait changes across chapters. The main thing is, you can expect that in the harder stories you're reading now, your characters will be harder to pin down."

Then, you might encourage these readers to innovate ways to trace their character's traits and emotions, and leave them to invent these ways, telling them you'll return soon. Go to another small group, then return in a bit to see how they've decided to set up their annotating/thinking work.

Support readers in lower-midlevel texts where characters are less complicated.

Some kids may be reading books like *Diary of a Wimpy Kid*, where at first glance, the characters may not seem very complicated. Greg, for instance, might initially seem one-dimensional. But if you read these stories, there is interesting work to do, sorting out the character's emotions or feelings, versus traits. Greg is often bitter and always clever.

You might coach some readers in these lower-level texts in the work of weighing and evaluating traits versus emotions. You can also coach them to use literary language and practice using word charts that students (and you) have been creating. You might create and show a couple of examples, such as a notebook page that appears to have been created over several days of reading, which also show students using the literary word charts.

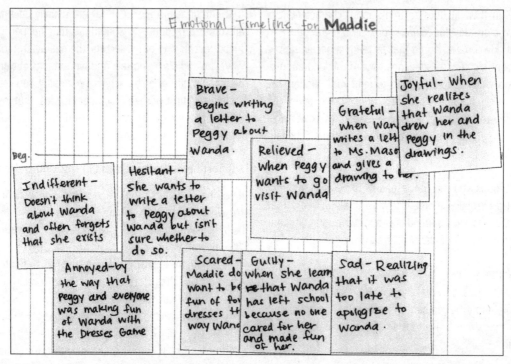

FIG. 4–3 An Emotional TImeline explains changes in character's feelings using literary language.

SHARE

Reflecting with Partners on Strongest Entries in Their Reading Notebooks

Ask partners to think about how they are using their notebooks to deepen their thinking.

"Readers, today you continued to think about the characters in your books. You learned that it is important to allow yourself to be conflicted over a character, to see the parts of a character that may not be the most admirable. And more than that, you have tried to write in ways that help you think deeply about characters.

"In a moment, you're going to have a chance to share with your partner. Will you look over your writing about reading and will you star the place where you think you have done your best thinking recently—the entry you think is most compelling? And then, can you and your partner take a moment to reflect, asking yourself, 'How am I using my notebook in innovative ways, to deepen my thinking?'"

If students are reading digitally, then many will also choose to annotate digitally. Their reading notebooks, then, will be places where they are sketching, charting, and writing longer entries.

SESSION 4 HOMEWORK

GETTING ENOUGH READING DONE—AND NOTICING A CHARACTER'S LESS LIKEABLE TRAITS

Readers, a few days ago, you saw how many pages you can read in thirty minutes, and you have been reading at least that amount—at least that amount—each night. For tonight's reading work, will you again time yourself, reading thirty minutes? But this time, I want to tell you that researchers suggest that in thirty minutes, you should be able to read at least twenty to thirty pages. So time yourself for thirty minutes, and see if, in that amount of time, you can read at least twenty pages. That might take pushing yourself to read a bit faster. Of course, you won't be thinking about speed as you read—you'll be thinking about the story. If you find, at thirty minutes, that you're not at twenty pages, keep reading until you are. To be able to read harder, longer books, it's going to be important that you begin to think about pages, rather than minutes, as you read. So push yourself to get to between twenty and thirty pages tonight.

Then after you read, use your notebook to develop or capture your thinking for four or five minutes. We've talked a lot about growing theories of your characters, including their bad sides. You can do that work tonight if you want, but you can do *any* thinking work that the book makes you do. Find a way to capture your best, deepest, most important thinking by writing after you read. You can write a timeline, a flowchart, a T-chart, a sketch, a freewriting entry: write or sketch something that captures your thinking.

Session 5

Read-Aloud

Some Character Traits Matter More Than Others, Because They Affect the Rest of the Story

GETTING READY

- Prepare your read-aloud (we read "Popularity" by Adam Bagdasarian, from *First French Kiss*) by noting places in the text where you will demonstrate a strategy, or later in the text, where you'll prompt students to practice that strategy. You'll also want to anticipate coaching or feedback you'll give as students try the work.
- Convene students for the read-aloud, each with a partner, some Post-its, and a reading notebook.
- Display your trait Post-it charts (from Session 1) and theory charts (from Session 2) (see Connection).
- Prepare to listen to partner talk, deciding whether the suggested feedback is relevant for them. You might also give feedback that celebrates—names and compliments—the work students are doing well (see Conducting the Read-Aloud).
- Display two traits on large Post-its, inside an arrow pointing to another Post-it that says, "What happens?" Display a second version of this chart as indicated in the text (see Conducting the Read-Aloud).
- Display and add to the anchor chart, "To Think Deeply about Characters" (see Link).

IN THIS SESSION

TODAY YOU'LL read aloud the second half of "Popularity" by Adam Bagdasarian, from *First French Kiss*. You will teach students that readers begin to realize that some character traits matter more than others, because they affect the rest of the story.

TODAY YOUR STUDENTS will learn to evaluate and choose which character traits matter the most to what happens in the story. They will use Post-its to revise their original theories about the character's traits, and will jot about links between traits and plot events in their notebooks.

CONNECTION

Before the read-aloud, follow through on last night's homework regarding the pace of kids' reading.

"Readers, last night you timed yourself to read for thirty minutes, and you noted the number of pages you read in that time. Would you and your partner talk about what happened for you when you did that?"

The room erupted into talk. After a minute or two, I said, "If you found it hard to read twenty pages in thirty minutes and had to keep reading, will you stay in the meeting area after we do some reading aloud, so we can think together about next steps for you? It's fabulous that you kept reading—that kind of determination will take you far. There are techniques for reading faster that I'd love to share with you."

Introduce the work of this read-aloud. Explain that readers begin to realize that some character traits influence the storyline and therefore matter more than others. Launch an investigation.

"Readers, today we're going to continue reading aloud. So far, we've been investigating how characters reveal their character traits over time in more complicated stories. We've seen that often characters will display several traits, some less likeable than others. We've also seen that sometimes our thinking changes as our knowledge of the character deepens, or as the character evolves."

I pointed to the earlier set of Post-its we had made, when we first read the story, and our theory charts.

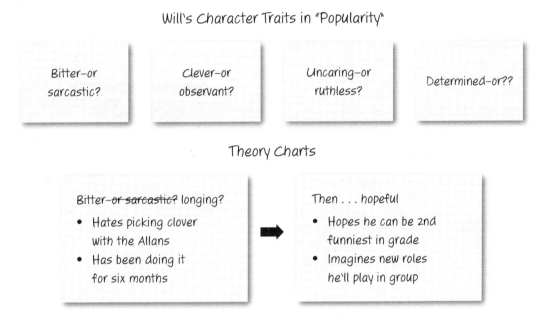

For middle school readers, identifying character traits should not be that hard, although as characters in their books become less static, it takes longer to make decisions about traits. One way to complicate their work (and make it more challenging) is to consider how some traits are not only more visible, they are more important. For instance, in The Hunger Games, *it's interesting to think about whether Katniss' compassion or her ruthlessness are more important to what happens.*

"Today, readers, I invite you to consider another lens on character traits—that often in stories, certain traits matter more than others, because they influence what happens in the story.

"As an example, think about *The Hunger Games*. If we think about how Katniss is so distrustful, that wasn't such a big deal in Book One when all that this influenced was whether or not she believed Gale or Peeta loved her. But in Book Two, her inability to trust gets people killed. Tributes who are trying to protect her end up dying for her, because she can't trust that they would be anything but enemies. That one character trait begins to shape everything that happens in the story.

"So today, I thought we could try that reading work together, reading in such a way that we investigate how some traits become particularly significant to the story overall—how they influence what happens in the rest of the story."

SESSION 5: READ-ALOUD

I pointed back to our Post-its and theory charts. "If you were to theorize right now, which of these traits would you predict might influence the rest of the plot the most? Think for a moment and compare with your partner—try to explain your theory."

I listened as partners mulled over Will's traits and developed theories that his determination would probably be significant, because it would help him get accepted. Others thought that ruthlessness or cleverness might matter more.

"Interesting! Some of you think Will's determination might most influence what happens, because Will won't give up on popularity. Others think it might be his ruthlessness, because he'll sacrifice anyone, like the Allans. A few are wondering if it might actually be how clever he is, if he'll figure out how to be popular because he's smart. What's great about what you're doing is how you're adding 'because . . .' That shows you're thinking about reasons and evidence to support your theories.

"Let's see. Let's go back to the story."

CONDUCTING THE READ-ALOUD

Reread a bit of the story, modeling how you focus your thinking about a character's traits that might end up being important to the story.

"When we left off, Will had been studying the popular crowd, especially Sean Owens, the athlete and uber-popular boy, and his sidekick, Mitch. We left it at a kind of ominous paragraph. Let's reread that, thinking not just about any traits we notice, but the ones that might end up being significant to what happens later. They may be ones you've already theorized about and jotted down."

I read aloud.

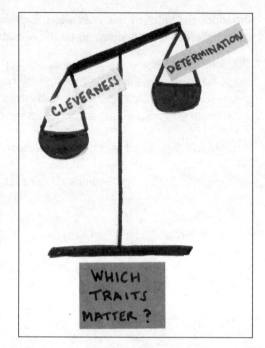

FIG. 5–1   Which of Will's traits influence the plot?

> I returned to the group every recess, for three days. I stood, unnoticed, just outside the outer circle, waiting for my moment, for the one joke or wisecrack that would make me popular. I knew that I would only get one chance to prove myself, and that if I failed, I would be sent back to the stables. And so, with the single-mindedness of a scientist, I listened to the jokes the other boys made, hoping to align my comic sensibilities with theirs. Now and then I found myself on the verge of saying something, but every time I opened my mouth to speak, Mitch would launch into another routine, and my moment passed, and I had to resign myself to yet another day in the dark.
>
> I did not know then that popularity has a life span, and that Mitch's time was about to run out.

"Hmm, . . . are you thinking what I'm thinking? These text details, about (I reread) going 'back to the stables,' and listening 'with the single-mindedness of a scientist,' and 'waiting for my moment . . . that would make me popular,' and . . . resigning himself 'to yet another day in the dark'—these seem to particularly reinforce Will's . . . cleverness? And . . . determination?" I waited for nods.

"I think I'm going to investigate these two traits. You might choose these, or stick with the ones you just talked over with a partner. Jot down the traits you most want to investigate either on Post-its or in your notebook, in a way that will help you keep track of them as the story unfolds."

I dashed these two traits up on large Post-its, inside an arrow pointing to another Post-it that said, ". . . what happens?"

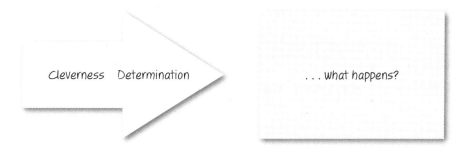

Channel students to continue to think more deeply about which traits become significant. Emphasize that they have to be partially in charge of the read-aloud, noting moments when they need time to jot.

"You want to find out if one of the traits you're investigating takes on extra importance because it influences the plot. If you begin to see that happening, or you see another trait begin to become even more important, give a signal, and I'll give you a moment to jot. You're kind of in charge in this read-aloud."

I waited to make sure everyone had reading notebooks open, Post-its ready to jot.

Then I said, "Let's read on and investigate if one of these traits influences what happens in the story. Keep in mind this question, 'How does one or more of these traits particularly influence what happens?'"

I read on, pausing when students motioned for a moment to jot, after the line, "Boys, I give you Tweety Bird."

Inviting students to decide when to pause in the read-aloud helps create a sense of agency. Notice if they seem to have a strong sense of when certain character traits become important, or if you have to pretend someone signaled in order to pause! If no one signals, kids may need support connecting character development to plot development. Or they may be overdependent on their teacher to guide their decision making.

> It is a sad fact of life that the clothes a child wears and how he wears them often determine his rank in school society. I knew it, Sean Owens knew it, everyone in school knew it. So maybe it was carelessness, or temporary insanity, or a subconscious desire to step back into the stress-free shadows of anonymity that caused Mitch Brockman to wear a yellow shirt with a yellow pair of pants. He might have gotten away with it if I hadn't left for school that same morning unaware that one folded cuff of my jeans was noticeably lower than the other. As it was, the two of us were on a collision course that only one of us would survive.
>
> At recess on that fateful day, I took my customary place a foot from the popular boys (wondering if I would ever get a chance to prove myself) and listened to Mitch tell another variation of his story about the wiener mobile. I pretended to enjoy this story as much as the others, while my mind strayed to a dream world where I did not have to feel so out of place, and Mitch and Sean and I were the best of friends. And then, with a suddenness that jarred me back to reality, Mitch Brockman, a boy who had never noticed me, never seemed to know or care that I was alive, turned to me, pointed at my uneven pants, and said, "Someone needs a ruler."
>
> This was, perhaps, the wittiest remark he had ever made, and I froze. With four words he had devastated all my aspirations, defined me as a fool, and all but condemned me to a life of shame and obscurity. I could see my future, my boyhood itself, crumbling to dust, and as I heard the laughter and felt the heat of the spotlight upon me, I pointed at Mitch's yellow pants and shirt and said, "Someone else needs a mirror. You look like a canary." Then, with the grace of a magician's assistant, I raised my left arm in a presentational gesture and said, "Boys, I give you Tweety Bird."

Notice when partners signal they want to jot, and pause for them. You might summarize the critical moment, as a cue for some readers.

"Readers, I see you wanting to jot. I agree. Wow! Will found his moment, and now he has openly mocked Mitch, comparing him to the cartoon character, Tweety Bird! Go ahead, look at your Post-its. Are any of those traits influencing what's happening? Do you want to revise your theory? I think I want to revise mine slightly." I pointed to our original trait Post-its. "Is there another trait that seems extra important?"

As students jotted, I crossed out one of my Post-its, replacing "Determination" with "Ruthlessness."

Here's where you may be wondering, "If you knew you were going to say he's ruthless, why didn't we choose that trait at the start of the read-aloud?" We are trying to model that readers are constantly revising their thinking, searching for more precise language to describe characters.

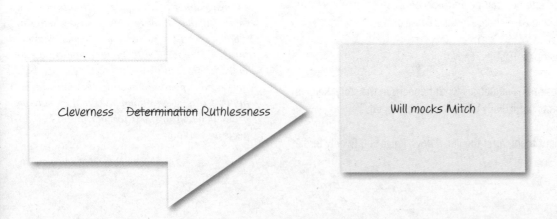

Then read on, pausing again at a dramatic moment in the plot ("The entire transformation was complete in a matter of months").

"I see some of you revising your theories, and some of you are sticking with one or both of the traits you listed as influential to what happens. Let's read on—and continue to weigh and evaluate which traits matter more than others. Give me a signal again if you want to pause."

I reread a bit and then read on until several students gestured, as expected, when Will begins to replace Mitch as Owen's sidekick.

> . . . I heard the laughter and felt the heat of the spotlight upon me, I pointed at Mitch's yellow pants and shirt and said, "Someone else needs a mirror. You look like a canary." Then, with the grace of a magician's assistant, I raised my left arm in a presentational gesture and said, "Boys, I give you Tweety Bird."
>
> And it was all over. As the volume of the laughter doubled, Mitch seemed to vanish, and that day, on that playground, Sean Owens's laughter was heard for the first time. In an instant, Mitch Brockman became Tweety Bird, and I, an absolute nonentity, became somebody. And then somebody special. Someone to seek out. Someone to follow. Sean Owens's first jester and best friend. The entire transformation was complete in a matter of months.

Our (or at least, my) generation is familiar with Tweety Bird. If that allusion would be lost on your students, you may want to show an image of this yellow cartoon character.

Once again, I summed up. "Huh, Will finally got what he wanted—he achieved popularity. Go ahead, do some jotting. I will as well." I added to my jots, writing about how Will replaces Mitch and the outcome, Will gets to be popular now.

Cleverness   ~~Determination~~ Ruthlessness
Will mocks   Will replaces Mitch
Mitch's clothes

→ Will gets to be popular now

SESSION 5: READ-ALOUD

Finish reading the story, then invite students to discuss their theories. Coach them to explain *how* a trait affected what happened in the story, by saying "because" and giving reasons and evidence.

"I can tell you're dying to talk. Let's finish the story. Add any jots that you need to develop your theory, and then you can discuss your theories with a partner. Be ready to really explain your theories."

I reread a little bit and then read on.

> During this time Mitch became a less and less vocal part of the group, telling fewer and fewer stories, until finally, the following year, he was gone—to another school perhaps, or another state, or another country. I never knew. No one knew because no one noticed—no one had called him for months. But *my* phone rang. *My* weekends were filled with sleep-overs and baseball games and bowling parties and bicycle races and more new friends than I knew what to do with.
>
> And I did not trust one of them, because I knew then that I was standing on sand and was only a yellow shirt and pair of pants away from the oak trees where the two Allans were still looking for four-leaf clovers.

"Wow, what an ending! I love how he brings it back to the two Allans, still looking for clovers. How chilling. I'm thinking about my theories. What about you? Jot your ideas, then discuss with your partner. How did certain traits affect what happens? Explain your theories, giving reasons and evidence."

I listened in as students talked, prompting them to think about cause and effect.

To one partnership, I said, "Your theory is that it's Will's cleverness that matters most? How did cleverness matter? How did it affect what happens?"

To another, "I like the way you are saying, 'because,' and giving reasons and evidence. You're explaining *how* the trait you named—'sarcastic'—ends up being important to the story. It was a nasty, sarcastic comment, wasn't it? Try to explain why it matters."

LINK

Invite students to try this work in their own books. Send them off to continue this work or to continue with prior thinking. Hold students who find it hard to read ¾ page to a page a minute.

"Readers, I added a point to our anchor chart, summing up what we just worked on. Keep this in mind as you read and think about your own books."

In your link, try to establish that students need to: make significant choices about their reading work; have a plan for that day's work; and develop their plans by considering the thinking work you are teaching in this bend of the unit. Negotiated choice!

> **ANCHOR CHART**
>
> To Think Deeply about Characters . . .
>
> - Expect characters to be complicated and show more than one trait.
> - Revise your thinking in the face of new evidence.
> - Look at a character's less likeable sides.
> - **Know that some traits matter more than others because they affect the rest of the story.**

Know that some traits matter more than others because they affect the rest of the story.

"Many of you are far enough along in your books that it can be interesting to think about which character traits seem especially influential. Or you could continue our earlier work, analyzing how characters are complicated, or their less likeable sides.

"Will you take a second and in your notebook, find a place to do some jotting about this, noting traits and plot events in your own book, and how they might be related? As always, make your writing brief and potent. It can be notes, diagrams, free writing, anything that works for you."

Kids worked quietly. I moved among them, appreciating those who opened their books to look back through it, and those whose notes seemed to actually hold thinking. After a minute or two, I whispered, "Off you go. You might continue this thinking today, or you may want to continue the thinking you were in the midst of already. You decide."

"Will those of you who found it hard to read twenty pages in half an hour stay here? Let's think about whether you might be thinking *too* deeply as you read! The rest of you, back to your reading spots."

INDEPENDENT READING

Supporting Students to Increase Reading Volume and to Draw on Repertoire

Your first job will be to note the students who struggled to read ¾ page a minute. You might point out to them that some researchers suggest that students sometimes worry about missing something and end up rereading twenty times within even just one page—they read forward, then reread, then read forward. Ask them to sit around you and to read quietly, trying to hold onto the story, but to *not reread* as they progress down the page. Move among them and do some quick assessing. "Will you read aloud, wherever you are?" you can say. Listen for whether their prosody suggests they comprehend the text. Is their fluency and phrasing compromised? It is not always the case that robotic-sounding reading suggests the book is too hard—some middle school readers, who came to reading later, may have never worked on fluency, but they do comprehend. Often, however, a lack of fluency is accompanied by a lack of accuracy, and the sum total adds up to a book that is too hard. In those instances, don't hesitate to bring readers to somewhat easier and shorter books, suggesting to them that switching to books they can read faster will help them get tons more reading done.

As always on read-aloud days, you won't have much time for conferring or small groups. You might check in at students' tables to support them in drawing upon a repertoire as they read. You might ask a few kids at the table about their work, then give quick, pointed compliments that support repertoire. Speak so others at the table can overhear and learn from your compliments. For example, you might say:

- "You're showing a real willingness to revise your thinking about characters as you gather new evidence about them. That will continue to be important as the characters evolve and perhaps less likeable traits emerge."

- "It's great that you are acknowledging more than one side of your character—you've recognized there may be a secretive side that's not as obvious as her bold, brash behavior. It will be interesting to see if this trait becomes significant to what happens in the story!"

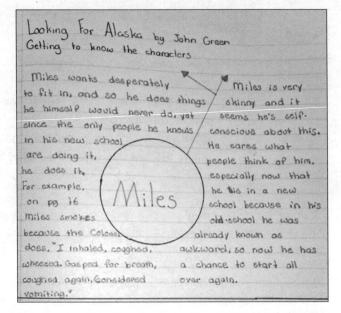

FIG. 5–2 Investigating physical and mental character traits

SHARE

Invite readers to decide on specific reading work to do for homework, then share those plans in partnerships.

"Readers, time is short so take a second to think, 'What reading work should I be doing tonight?' You can use our anchor chart, your knowledge of the genre, and your partner to help you plan. In your reader's notebook tonight, write yourself a self-assignment, and then, tonight, do the work you assign for yourself."

SESSION 5 HOMEWORK

FOLLOWING THROUGH ON PLANS FOR READING WORK

In today's reading workshop, you committed to a plan for your reading work. Tonight, follow through on your plan. You'll share your reader's notebooks with your partner tomorrow.

In addition, make sure you are reading a lot. Your goal is to begin to read between thirty and forty minutes a night, which will mean between twenty and forty pages. Of course, keep reading more when you can!

Session 6

Lifting the Level of Your Writing about Reading

IN THIS SESSION

TODAY YOU'LL teach students several tips to help them lift the level of their writing about reading.

TODAY YOUR STUDENTS will read on in their books, drawing on a repertoire of work to help them think more deeply about characters. They will write short or long about their reading for a brief amount of time, depending on their fluency and aims, using tips to set goals and improve the quality of their writing about reading.

GETTING READY

- Ask students to bring their writing about reading homework to the meeting area (see Connection).
- Display a list of "Tips for Taking Your Writing about Reading from Good to Great." You will reveal tips, one by one (see Teaching, Active Engagement, and Link).
- For gallery walk, students will need their notebooks to display their writing about reading. Provide stacks of Post-its (see Share).
- Provide students with mini-copies of charts, "Tips for Taking Your Writing about Reading from Good to Great" and "Thinking Deeply about Characters" (see Homework).

MINILESSON

CONNECTION

Channel partners to share the writing about reading they each did for homework last night.

I asked students to gather in the meeting area with the writing about reading they did for homework. "Will you take a minute or two to give your partner a tour of the writing about reading you did last night? Show your partner what you jotted and explain why you chose to jot that particular information." While students shared, I circulated, noting who had completed their homework and common characteristics of that homework.

Share feedback on students' entries. Explain that a few small tips can help students lift the level of their writing about reading, which in turn will lead to higher-level thinking.

"I'm noticing something big as I look across your writing about reading. It looks like a lot of you are doing something I find myself doing sometimes for my book club, if I'm sort of rushed, or don't love the book—or sometimes it's that I love the book and don't want to pause. That is, you are recording what you're thinking in the moment, jotting down whatever's in your head. That type of writing about reading just doesn't help you to think more deeply about your reading. Your book deserves better thinking, your partner does, and you do."

❖ **Name the teaching point.**

"Today I want to teach you that the strongest writing about reading actually lifts the level of your thinking about the book. Whenever you pause in your reading to do some writing, it helps to think about how you want to capture not your first thinking, but your best thinking."

TEACHING

Introduce a series of tips about lifting the level of writing about reading, elaborating on each tip you share.

"Can I share some tips with you that will help you really take your writing about reading from good to great, so that your writing about reading helps you to think more deeply about what you're reading? Great! Listen closely, because in a few minutes you'll study your own writing about reading to decide which things you're already doing and which should be your goals."

I revealed a new chart, "Tips for Taking Your Writing about Reading from Good to Great." As I introduced each tip, I revealed it on our chart.

"Our goal is to move from jotting the first thinking that comes to mind—and instead, capture our *best* thinking. Here are some tips for how to do that without it taking forever.

"My first tip: The time you spend reading matters above all. Your writing about reading should just take up a small percentage of your time. Researchers at Columbia University say you should 'only spend ten percent of your reading time writing. Prioritize quality over quantity.' That means you'll want to only jot your most interesting, nuanced thinking.

"Here's tip two: Don't jot the things you can remember. If you can remember how all the characters are connected, don't jot that down. You want to only jot things that you can't hold in your head, like ideas you are investigating.

"Are you already thinking about which of these you do as a writer about reading?

FIG. 6–1 These kinds of annotations or Post-its suggest that the reader is recording first thinking, rather than best-thinking. Move students to jotting about what they are uncertain of, what they theorize but still need to investigate, or what other readers might miss. No more random Post-its.

The Carnegie Center for Educational Excellence published a study, "Writing to Read," that you can access online. It suggests that writing about reading increases students' comprehension, retention, and interpretation.

"Here's another tip: Don't start jotting too quickly or automatically. Don't record your first thoughts. Record your most interesting thoughts. That means before you jot down your first thought, think, 'So what?' or 'What this makes me think is . . .' and push yourself to even richer thinking.

"The last tip: Decide what kind of writing best suits your thinking. If you own the book, annotate in it, marking up lines and jotting thoughts as you go. If you don't own the book, jot a quick Post-it. To trace an idea over time, create a sketch, a timeline, or a chart, or combine Post-its with any of those. When you get an idea that needs to grow, one you need to think more about, you might write long in your notebook."

ACTIVE ENGAGEMENT

Rally students to study their writing about reading and to set a goal for how to lift the level of their writing about reading moving forward. Set partners up to share observations and goals.

"Will you pull out your writing about reading and study it with these tips in mind? What have you already done to lift the level of your writing about reading? Once you know what tips you've already tried, think about which tips should be goals for you as you write about your reading over the next few days."

I gave students a minute to study their writing about reading independently, and then said, "Your partner already knows what you jotted about and why. This time, share which tips you've already tried out and which will become goals for you."

While partnerships talked, I coached in:

- "Point to places in your writing about reading where you applied that tip."
- "Be tough on yourself. If you only *sometimes* do something, it probably needs to be a goal for you."
- "Tell your partner *how* you'll work on those goals."

Name out a few goals students set for themselves.

"You're setting big goals to lift the level of your writing about reading. In one partnership, a student realized she's been writing everything—all her first thoughts, all the things she can hold in her head—and she needs to scale back on her writing about reading so it's just 10% of her reading time. Her partner realized she hardly ever jots and she sometimes forgets ideas she had while reading. She realized that if she forces herself to pause at the end of each chapter, she might find she has something worth jotting. They are both going to take not only their writing about reading but their thinking about reading from good to great!"

Tips for Taking Your Writing about Reading from Good to Great ✓

- Spend 10% of your reading time writing. Prioritize quality over quantity.
- Only jot things you can't hold in your head.
- Don't record your first thought. Record your most interesting thoughts.
- Decide what kind of writing best suits your thinking.
    - Annotations in the margins
    - Post-it notes
    - Creating a table/sketch/diagram in your notebook
    - Writing fast, furious, long

LINK

Restate the teaching point. Remind students that they should spend the vast majority of their reading time reading, only pausing to write for a few minutes.

"Remember that whenever you sit down to read, whenever you stop to jot, you can make the decision to do particularly strong writing about reading, to write in ways that actually lift the level of your thinking. You've set some powerful goals that will help you take your writing from good to great.

"As you go off to read and write today, will you especially keep in mind that first tip? Your writing about reading should just take up 10% of your reading time. That means that most of the thinking work you do about your characters today will be in your head, and your best thinking will make it into your notebook." I added this point to our "Tips for Taking Your Writing about Reading from Good to Great" chart.

Remind students of the connection between writing about reading and partnerships, and introduce a meeting place for impromptu partner conversations.

"Readers, another really important purpose of writing about your reading is to hold onto ideas that you want to share with a partner or a club. Today and going forward, as you read, will you be thinking about the fact that your writing is a way to prepare for having better conversations with your partner?

CONFERRING AND SMALL-GROUP WORK

Matching Students' Writing about Reading to Their Reading Work and Attending to Balance

TODAY, YOU MIGHT CONSIDER helping students to take their writing about reading from good to great. It's a tricky balance, as you always want most of the time that kids put into reading to be put into *reading*. We say to kids, "Read for thirty to forty minutes, write for three to four minutes . . . read for sixty minutes, write for five to six minutes." You want kids to develop the habit of annotating or jotting every now and then, so that they document and expand their thinking, going for quality over quantity. They only need to document thinking that they can't hold in their head. Ultimately, kids' writing about reading will be a window into the thinking work they are doing as they read, and you're looking for a close match between your instruction and the work kids are doing. More significant time for writing about reading, such as drafting for literary essays, will happen during writing workshop. Following are options for possible conferences and small groups to support writing about reading in these early days.

Kids Who Resist Jotting, Acting Like It Will Be the Death of Reading to Do Any Annotation

Some kids, often avid readers, hate to jot. They read fast and furiously, often remember their books well, and don't want to slow down to write anything down. When you and I read a lot, it's true that we don't jot about every page, or every chapter, or even every book, or maybe any book, so we tend to have sympathy for these kids.

Yet there are important reasons to compel these readers to slow down to capture their thinking. One is that sometimes they are reading avidly, but not thinking that deeply. They find the plot compelling, but they miss some of the nuances. Those readers deserve to grow as much as any other student. You want to do everything possible to make sure those readers are engaged in deliberate practice of the new thinking work. Another reason is that kids think they will remember exactly what they were thinking when they put down a book—but they go to soccer or science, and all that rich thinking leeches away.

So you might pull together some of your strong, fast readers into a small group. You might say, "You read fast and don't want to pause. But the depth and richness of your thinking need to be as evident as your pace. You should be having even more nuanced and complicated partner talks than other readers and be able to show how your thinking has changed across a book, but sometimes, your thinking is . . . rather thin. You need to take a moment every now and then, and definitely before you close a book, to capture your most nuanced, interesting thinking—in a quick margin annotation, a jot in your notebook, or a series of Post-its. I'm not saying take a lot of time. But make those three minutes count—write about stuff that other readers might miss. Read for forty minutes, jot for three minutes."

Readers Who Are Jotting, But Their Jottings Have Little to Do with Strategies You Are Teaching in Class

Many kids listen politely during minilessons, even try out new work in read-aloud, and then, in their independent work, they revert to work they were doing before new instruction. You'll know this when you see kids writing Post-its like "Amber Brown is mad" or "Katniss is scared" when the book and chapter titles make that obvious. Look closely at what kids are jotting. Consider if it shows evidence of the thinking work you've been teaching.

Sometimes you may need to lure these kids into higher-level work. You might say, "As the stories you read become more complicated and sophisticated, your thinking work needs to be equally complicated and sophisticated. It's not hard reading work for you to recognize that Katniss is scared, or Triss is tough. So you might push yourself to see not just the traits on the surface, but also look for ones that might take longer to see. And definitely push to do that work of looking for the source of those traits. It will ensure that you are really pushing yourself to do harder thinking. Let's look at how you're using your notebooks, what kind of jotting you're doing. Let's see if you might do something harder and more complicated . . ."

After giving students a minute to look over their notebooks, you might say, "You could come up with a new way of taking notes to help get to the higher-level thinking that goes along with the kinds of books you're reading. For example, to track a character's traits over time, you might make a timeline to record traits, with evidence for each trait. Or find a way to sort traits into categories showing likeable and less likeable sides of the character. Another thing you might do is have two columns, one showing traits on the inside and one on the outside, and see if any of these shift over. For instance, I think how Katniss tries to be tough on the outside all the time, and perhaps, over time, she also becomes tough on the inside."

Then you might channel students to share new ways to set up their notes that would lead to higher-level thinking. Once students have a plan, send them off. Remind them to check their note-taking systems from time to time to make sure their writing about reading reflects the complex thinking work their books call for.

You'll note that this is just a much more appealing way of saying, "I'm teaching you hard, new stuff, and you're doing easy, old stuff." Most kids respond to the urge to be more sophisticated and complicated.

Kids Who Are Writing Way Too Much, Making Art Projects or Literary Essays Out of Every Bit of Thinking

Some kids will be making a religion of writing about reading. They seem to have 10,000 Post-its for their first book, taped in order in their notebook. Or they've made complicated, multicolored diagrams and sketches, all visually appealing and time-consuming.

Or they take every preliminary idea and turn it into a mini-literary essay, developing claims, reasons, and evidence. In general, not more than 10% of a reader's reading time should be spent writing about reading—and you want to convey that and negotiate that in respectful ways. Today you rallied your students to work toward this goal.

You don't want to turn these kids away from achievement. Research them for a bit. Invite them to research themselves. "My writers-about-reading," you might say, "I admire the extraordinary volume and completeness in your reading notebooks. Some of you are making incredible sketches and diagrams. Some of you are writing little essays. Some of you seem to capture all your thinking on many Post-its. Now I want you to shift a bit to think about quality versus quantity. Consider two possibilities. One is sustainability. You're going to do a lot of reading this year. Make sure you're getting a brilliant balance between reading a ton and capturing your thinking. The second possibility is that it might be worth it to read bigger chunks of text before deciding what's worth thinking about. Maybe sometimes, you've put real effort into documenting some initial thinking, but had you read another fifty pages, you might not have considered it so important and you'd have a more nuanced idea later."

Pose these questions as an inquiry, and kids will usually begin to readjust on their own, or in consultation with their partners. If you tell them to cut back, they may cut too far back, or lose their zeal. The tone you want is "reader to reader, writer to writer, what are some of the real issues that we struggle with?" It's not the notebook itself that matters, it's the thinking work that kids are doing that matters.

SHARE

A Gallery Walk to Study Writing about Reading

Ask students to display their writing about reading. Then, invite students to study the writing about reading, noting ways in which their classmates have taken their work from good to great.

"Readers, I've had the chance to look at a ton of your notebooks today as I've been circulating around the room. Before we leave today, I want you to have the opportunity to do the same thing. Will you make a quick display of your writing about reading on your desk? Open up your notebook, lay out your Post-it notes, or flag pages where you did some purposeful annotating."

Once students had their displays set up, I said, "Grab a stack of Post-it notes. Now that your gallery exhibit is set up, will you move from desk to desk studying your classmates' writing about reading? What did your classmates do to take their writing from good to great? Jot what you're noticing on your Post-it notes so you can try those same moves next time you write about your reading."

SESSION 6 HOMEWORK

THINK DEEPLY ABOUT CHARACTERS, THEN SHARPEN YOUR WRITING ABOUT READING

Tonight, I'm sending you home with mini-copies of two charts, "Tips for Taking Your Writing about Reading from Good to Great" and "Thinking Deeply about Characters." Tonight, will you aim to read for at least forty minutes (which should mean you read at least thirty pages)? As you read, you'll want to be doing rich character work in your mind, determining which traits are most dominant, rethinking a character's traits as you read on, and considering your character's less likeable sides. When you do pause to jot for four to five minutes, make the most of it. Work on the goals you set in class today. Use some of the moves you saw in your classmates' work in today's gallery walk.

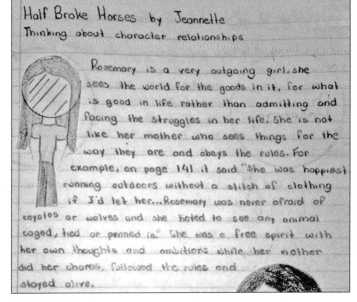

FIG. 6–2 Students can be inspired to be more playful in their notebooks.

Session 7

Readers Consider the Pressures Acting on Characters

GETTING READY

- Display a moment/scene from the video clip you showed earlier from *Harry Potter and the Half-Blood Prince*, Sectumsempra scene. A link to the video is available in the online resources. (see Connection).
- You'll return to your read-aloud text, so have it available to review (see Teaching).
- Students should bring their novels to the minilesson (see Active Engagement and Link).
- Display and add to anchor chart, "To Think Deeply about Characters" (see Link).
- Provide mini-copies of chart, "Questions to Pressure Partners to Deepen Their Thinking," to students (see Share and Homework).

IN THIS SESSION

TODAY YOU'LL teach students to consider pressures on characters that might cause them to behave in less-than-likeable ways. Readers do this by returning to scenes where the behavior emerges and analyzing possible causes.

TODAY YOUR STUDENTS will consider the link between pressures on characters and behavior, using the read-aloud text and personal experiences. Then they will bring this thinking to their books.

MINILESSON

CONNECTION

Return to an example of a character acting in less likeable ways. Show students how considering pressures on the character may help to understand the character's actions.

"Readers, I've continued to think about the work we did the other day, where we pushed ourselves to think how a perceptive reader acknowledges a character's less likeable traits. It's not easy seeing all the parts of people."

I put the image of Harry cursing Malfoy back on the screen.

"A researcher named Pedro Noguera studies teens. He says that when teens act in problematic ways, it's often because there are pressures acting on them. When pressures become unbearable, Noguera says, it can cause kids to become deceptive or destructive. That's sort of what we saw with Harry yesterday."

Pedro Noguera's City Schools and the American Dream *looks at, among other things, what happens to kids when the pressures from school, family, and peers conflict.*

"Here's the thing, friends. Some of you who are Harry Potter experts came to me later, and you wanted to explain more about what led to that scene where Harry almost kills Malfoy. You were talking about all sorts of circumstances, like Harry was trying to stop Malfoy from hurting another student, and that Harry was being influenced by the sorcerous book he was reading.

"Which brings me to this idea: sometimes things are more complicated than they seem. It's important to see the less likeable sides of characters, and it's also important to be empathetic, to try to understand what leads characters to do the things they do."

♣ **Name the teaching point.**

"Readers, today I want to teach you that characters have reasons for the things they do and the ways they are. It's helpful for a reader to ask, 'What pressures might there be on this character? Do those pressures help me understand the character's actions and decisions?'"

FIG. 7–1   A Pressure Map for Harry Potter

TEACHING

Invite readers to consider the less likeable sides of the protagonist from the read-aloud text, and then to consider possible pressures that explain these sides.

"Readers, I want to show you something, but first, can you think of a way in which our character, Will, is not all that likeable?" I left a bit of silence. "You'll be thinking of a less-than-admirable trait."

"Nod when you have a not-so-likeable part of Will in mind." I waited a moment for them to nod.

Demonstrate by reconsidering the pressures that Will experiences in "Popularity." Engage students in thinking alongside you.

"I think Will can be pretty ruthless, or cruel. Do you agree? Okay, let's go with that. First, let's think of some examples of when he's ruthless, like when he ditches the Allans, even though they have been his only company for months. Or when he calls Mitch 'Tweety Bird,' and gets the other kids to laugh at him. That was pretty ruthless. Let me reread that part, and see if you agree with me."

> *. . . I heard the laughter and felt the heat of the spotlight upon me, I pointed at Mitch's yellow pants and shirt and said, "Someone else needs a mirror. You look like a canary." Then, with the grace of a magician's assistant, I raised my left arm in a presentational gesture and said, "Boys, I give you Tweety Bird."*
>
> *And it was all over. As the volume of the laughter doubled, Mitch seemed to vanish, and that day, on that playground, Sean Owens's laughter was heard for the first time. In an instant, Mitch Brockman became Tweety Bird, and I, an absolute nonentity, became somebody. And then somebody special. Someone to seek out. Someone to follow. Sean Owens's first jester and best friend. The entire transformation was complete in a matter of months.*

During this time Mitch became a less and less vocal part of the group, telling fewer and fewer stories, until finally, the following year, he was gone—to another school perhaps, or another state, or another country. I never knew. No one knew because no one noticed—no one had called him for months. But my phone rang. My weekends were filled with sleep-overs and baseball games and bowling parties and bicycle races and more new friends than I knew what to do with.

I waited for nods. "Yup, he's ruthless! He gets all the other boys to laugh at Mitch, which pretty much destroys Mitch. So . . . let's ask ourselves the question Pedro Noguera suggests we ask: What pressures might the character be under? What might be driving him to act this way?"

"I see you've got ideas. Now turn and talk. What pressures are on Will? What explains his behavior?"

Let students share their thinking with each other, then gather them to recap.

I gave students a minute to talk, then called for their attention. "Readers, I'm listening to you and we are thinking a lot of the same things. The biggest pressure we're all talking about is the pressure to be popular. That is huge, and it's driving Will to be mean and heartless. It seems like this is the kind of school where only popular kids count. They're the only ones who get to play tag or have any fun.

"Some of you talked about the pressure of loneliness, how that too might be making Will ruthless. Because he doesn't have any real friends, he's looking for approval from this crowd. That's so interesting.

"Also, I wonder about one more thing. I wonder how ruthless Mitch had just been, when he said that Will needed a ruler because his pants were too short. So maybe the pressure of *other* kids being cruel is making Will cruel as well? Were some of you wondering about that?"

Review the steps you followed to grow your thinking about the character.

"Readers, did you see how we thought of a trait that we didn't love about a main character? And then we rethought the story so far, thinking about scenes where that trait emerges and pressures that are on the character, that might explain that trait? It's interesting thinking work. It gives you new insights into characters—it might even make you more sympathetic to unlikeable characters in general."

ACTIVE ENGAGEMENT

Give students a chance to transfer this thinking to their own lives.

"Let's give you a chance to try this thinking out—not just in your novels, but in your lives. Pedro Noguera suggests that most teens and preteens feel a variety of pressures, and some of those pressures might be conflicting. You might have pressure from friends to be one way, and pressure from parents to be another way. Those pressures might influence your behavior, and might even, at times, cause you to behave in ways that are less than likeable.

Noguera's research suggests that when school and peer norms don't coincide, peer pressure will almost always dominate. Thinking about characters in novels, then, becomes a way to think about the very real pressures that are exerted on readers in their all-too-real daily lives. Eve Sedgwick suggests that readers are implicitly learning from fictional characters as they read. We learn how we want to be and not be.

"One reason that we read is to learn from the books that we're reading, to come back to our own lives with more insight. So take a moment and think about a time when you behaved in a not-so-likeable way."

After a moment, I said, "Now think, were there pressures exerted on you that might have caused you to act this way? I know, it may be difficult to talk about these things. It takes a lot of courage to acknowledge when we act in ways we're not so proud of. When you have an idea, turn and talk."

I gave students a minute to talk, then called them back.

"Readers, this is intriguing! I heard some of you talking about times you snapped at your parents or at your friends. I heard about borrowing a sibling's things without asking, and about not taking care of yourself, like not eating right or getting enough sleep. Some of you said you weren't so nice to someone, maybe to fit in, like Will. You are brave to talk of these times. It's not easy to look at a moment we're not proud of.

"I also heard you talking about some causes of these behaviors, like pressures to do well in school—or pressures to wear certain fashions or to be good at sports. Many also talked about popularity—how it can feel like it matters, even if you don't want it to. Yikes! I wish I could make these pressures better for you.

"Like Will, we're all going to be shaped by these pressures. Thinking about them might help us make more positive decisions than Will does. It may also help us forgive each other for when we do slip up, as Will did."

LINK

Review choices readers have for assigning themselves reading work, and send them off when they have clear plans.

ANCHOR CHART

To Think Deeply about Characters . . .

- Expect characters to be complicated and show more than one trait.
- Revise your thinking in the face of new evidence.
- Look at a character's less likeable sides.
- Know that some traits matter more than others because they affect the rest of the story.
- **Consider the pressures exerted on characters.**

Consider the pressures exerted on characters.

"Readers, will you look over our anchor chart and think for a moment about which bullets represent work that will be especially important when you are at the beginning of a book? (And I know many of you are beginning your second book, so that work will be good for you to be doing today.) Which of this work is especially important in the middle of books? At the end of books?" I left a moment of silence.

"I'm asking you to look back over this whole chart because on any one day, we'll be thinking about a new kind of work that readers do related to growing deeper ideas about characters. But in the end, your book and your placement in that book (beginning, middle, end) and your goals will all challenge you toward doing some of this work. You don't want new reading work to just replace earlier reading work. It's more like when you get better at soccer—a new move makes your whole game better.

"If you aren't close to starting a new book, look at how many pages you're reading each day. If you're not getting enough reading done, ask yourself if you need to make more time to read or if you're spending too much time writing."

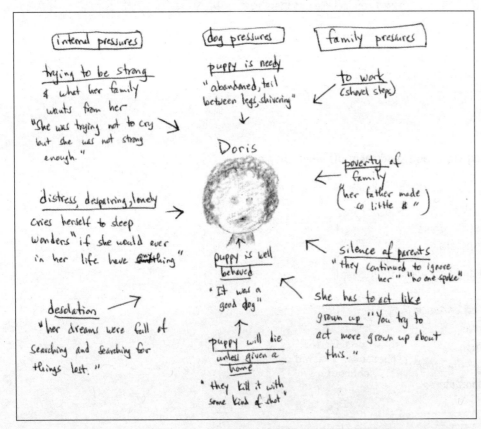

FIG. 7–2 This pressure map for "Stray" also includes specific text evidence.

CONFERRING AND SMALL-GROUP WORK

Supporting Purposeful Thinking and Talking about Texts

AT THIS POINT IN THE UNIT, students know and are hopefully drawing upon multiple ways to study characters as they read. Ideally, they are grounding their thinking in evidence from the text and bringing their thinking to their partner conversations.

As students' work and their novels grow in complexity, it can be daunting to know what to teach in a conference, particularly if you haven't read their books. Fortunately, you can have fabulous conferences even if you aren't familiar with the books, and at times even more so, because you'll focus your teaching on transferable strategies and not on the book's content. Here are a few ways to focus your coaching to support students at this point in the unit, even if you aren't familiar with the books they are reading.

Conferences and Small Groups to Support Students Grounding Their Thinking in the Text

Many students don't understand that grounding one's thinking in a text doesn't just mean recalling the plot outline of a novel to support an idea about the text. Instead, when readers are asked to ground their thinking in a text, they need to reread, to home in on relevant passages, to study and even annotate those passages. Looking closely at the text will spark new observations and new ideas. In conferences and small groups, you can help readers to come to a new understanding of what it means to base their thinking on evidence simply by bringing them back to specific parts and lines in the text.

This work is crucial. Many students are game to try on new kinds of big thinking after minilessons, but still struggle to ground their thinking in the text. As you confer, ask students to show you how they are supporting their thinking with evidence from the text. Coach them to cite specific parts and to explain how the actual words of the text are important to their thinking.

Conferences to Support Goal-Setting

A simple way to nudge students further along in their skill trajectory is to ask them to walk you through some of the ways they are trying to get better as readers. You might keep on hand mini-versions of the anchor chart to use as a checklist of sorts, and give students a moment or two to check off strategies they feel they are using regularly. You might do a spot check by asking them to show you multiple places where they used a particular strategy. Then, talk with them about what their next steps might be as a reader. For example, do they need more practice revising their thinking when they get new evidence? Or more practice weighing evidence to develop theories about dominant character traits? Jot the goal on a sticky note to leave with the student, or have the student record it as a visible reminder.

Conferences to Support Partnerships

You might use some of your conferring time today to check in on partnerships and ways that students aim to draw each other to do higher-level work. You might pop in on several partnerships, asking them to walk you through some of the thinking they are doing together, including any writing they may have done to prepare for partner talks. Note if they need support in exploring a line of thinking together, preparing for conversations by jotting notes or rehearsing, or making clear plans about what they will read together.

You might even call for the attention of the whole class at some point during independent reading time, and ask them to turn to their partners and share some of their latest insights. This will allow you to quickly scan their conversations and to note any that seem to be falling flat so you can step in to help.

SHARE

Pressuring Reading Partners to Deepen Their Thinking

Channel partners to ask each other questions to deepen thinking about their reading—significant new ideas, how these ideas develop in their books.

"Readers, today we thought about how characters are influenced by the pressures that are put on them, and sometimes those pressures tear them apart in different ways. That can be true for us, too, in our own lives—like when our family pressures us in one way, and peers or school pressures us in a different way. So we know that conflicting pressures, especially, can be damaging.

"But pressure, when it is challenging and supportive, can also be a good thing. You can pressure people to be kinder or nicer. Your coaches might pressure you in ways that help you perform better. And you can pressure your friends in ways that help them be smarter, deeper thinkers.

"Let's try it. Will you and your partner divide up so one of you is Partner 1, one of you is Partner 2?

"Partner 1, you are going to be the reader today, and Partner 2, you are going to be the questioner. Partner 1, will you ask Partner 2 a question—I'll suggest one. Then when your partner answers, listen and question in a way that pressures your partner to think more deeply, to justify his or her thinking, to develop ideas.

"Here's our starting question: 'What is the most important new idea or thinking you've been developing as you read?' Go ahead, Partner 1, talk a bit about your most significant idea or thinking."

I handed out versions of a mini-chart, and said, "Partner 2, here are some other questions that can help you pressure your partner. Try one of them out."

>
>
> **Questions to Pressure Partners to Deepen Their Thinking**
>
> ? What is the most significant new idea or thinking you've been developing as you read?
>
> ? Why does that idea feel important to the whole book?
>
> ? Where is the first place in the text that sparked that thinking?
>
> ? What passage or line is most important to this idea? Why is it significant?
>
> ? How has your thinking about this idea changed across the book? Why?
>
> ? Can you imagine someone arguing with that idea of yours? What might that person say? How might you respond?

After kids talked for a while, I said, "After this, will you try to listen in ways that pressure each other to be as thoughtful as possible? If you have ideas for ways to question each other—and yourselves, bring them up, and we'll add them to this chart."

I added, "Take home your copy of the mini-chart. You'll need those questions to do your homework tonight."

SESSION 7 HOMEWORK

 ### ASKING QUESTIONS TO DEEPEN YOUR OWN THINKING

Readers, tonight, after you read for thirty to forty minutes, will you use your notebook to have a dialogue about your thinking? Take the questions in your mini-chart that help you pressure a partner, and use them to deepen your own thinking. Ask yourself one or two of these questions, and then answer them. This will lead you to write between a page and a page and a half—but that writing needs to be fast. It should take five to seven minutes.

Session 8

Readers Reflect (on Their Novels and Their Reading Lives)

Dear Teachers,

Today marks the end of the first bend of the unit. It also marks the end of about two weeks of thoughtful reading work for your students, during which most kids have read more than one book, and some may have read a few. Your students have worked at being more conscious of how much they are reading and pushed themselves to read more. They've worked on making their thinking and talking about characters more insightful, and they've worked on using reading notebooks to deepen their thinking and their partner conversations. You've also pushed students to be more independent—to use tools like the anchor chart to remind themselves of reading work they might pursue, to set themselves to do independent homework, and to think of their reading as small courses of study.

This is a good day for helping your students step back and get some perspective—on their novels and on their reading lives. It's also a good time for you to consider each class with a more bird's-eye perspective, considering which partnerships are working and which may need to be renegotiated, which students are in books that are at that perfect outside edge of their zone of proximal development and which ones need your help to get on better courses of study.

Yesterday, you finished with students posing questions as a way to pressure their partners to deepen their thinking. They continued this work for homework, directing these questions at themselves and writing long in their notebooks. Have readers bring their books (the ones they are reading and if possible, any they have finished) and their notebooks to the lesson.

To begin today's work, as the connection to your minilesson, you might invite students to share their writing with a partner, reading bits of it aloud and talking about how they deepened their thinking about characters. Emphasize that what's most important is that now, at the end of this first bend in the unit, they have learned to push themselves and each other, using their writing about reading and their conversations.

Then move to how it's also a good time to think back over their novels. You might say, "The other day you thought about the reading work—specifically character work—that readers do at the start of books, in the middle of books, and near the end of books. Today we are at the end of our first bend in the unit. By now, most of you have come to the end of your first book (or certainly you are near the end of the first book). I thought we could spend some time thinking together about the sorts of thinking that readers often do at the end of their books." You might invite students to reflect on the insightful thinking work they've done at the end of their books. Make them laugh or groan when you share that, back in your time as a student, you had to write book reports, make posters, or build dioramas to show you had read the book.

Your teaching point might sound something like, "Today I want to teach you that when you reach the ending of a book, it is not unlike reaching the summit of a mountain climb. The ending of a book gives you perspective. It's valuable to linger there for a bit, and to look back on the trail you and the characters have traveled, seeing the whole of it." Then you might explain how, when you get to the top of a mountain hike or bike trail, you can look back, seeing all the tricky terrain, the streams and ravines. In the same way, when you look back over a novel from the perspective of the ending, new parts seem significant, and you have new insight into things about the characters and story that may have been confusing. You might demonstrate from the perspective of finishing the second book in The Hunger Games trilogy, *Catching Fire*, and how, like Katniss, you were somewhat confused about whom to trust and about each tribute's motives. But then, knowing at the end that Hamish and Peeta had been working with the game maker and other tributes toward two goals—protecting Katniss and breaking out of the Arena—all sorts of small moments make more sense. Show how you often find yourself going back to reread key parts, now that you know more.

Then invite students to do the same. It might be helpful to share a mini-chart, with some suggestions.

Then as you send students off to read, you might encourage them that this might be a day when it makes sense to reread, see new things, and choose spots with care that they want to write about in their notebooks and share with a partner. Suggest that today, they might want to reread, jot, or discuss, a few times. Meanwhile, add this strategy to your anchor chart.

Revisiting Key Parts of a Narrative from the Perspective of the Ending

* <u>The opening scene:</u> Are there details or clues that take on more meaning now?

* <u>Critical moments of decision:</u> Do some end up affecting what happens at the end?

* <u>Moments when minor characters become major players:</u> Were some moments with minor characters key to what happens?

* <u>Confusing details or allusions:</u> Were there references or details that didn't make sense, that become clear by the end?

* <u>Inspiring character actions:</u> Were there moments when characters inspired you?

ANCHOR CHART

To Think Deeply about Characters . . .

- Expect characters to be complicated and show more than one trait.
- Revise your thinking in the face of new evidence.
- Look at a character's less likeable sides.
- Know that some traits matter more than others because they affect the rest of the story.
- Consider the pressures exerted on characters.
- **Reflect on the characters and the story again, after you read the ending.**

For your conferring and small-group work, you may want to visit with kids about their reading lives. At this point in a unit, I like to visit with three kinds of readers: partnerships that need coaching or that need to be renegotiated; students who need support with their book choices; students who need a cheerleader or life coach to increase their reading volume.

I always try to take the end of a bend to do some quick fixing up and cementing of partnerships. One way I do this is to visit with partnerships that are going well, and document some of their traits. I do some research on how much reading they are getting done, how they are using their notebooks, what their reading logs look like. I listen to how they listen to and push each other. That becomes my vision for all my students. Then I visit with partnerships that don't necessarily need to change, but they need shoring up. They might be friendship partners, who need to push each other harder. For those students, I talk about the academic capital that comes with academic friendships, and I help them think through how they can help each other achieve. Finally, I talk to some kids, saying things like, "I've been thinking about you as a reader, and I've been thinking that you and so-and-so might be good reading partners, because . . ." My goal is to switch one or two partnerships as needed, and shore up others.

Then I try to get to the kids who seem to be reading books that are still too easy or too hard—the reader who is "reading" *The Maze Runner* who needs to be reading Gordon Korman novels, and the reader who is reading *Diary of a Wimpy Kid*, who could be reading *Maus*. I use my courses of study booklist to think of series or titles within the same genre, and do my best to get these students into books that will help them move up levels of complexity. I try to stay unafraid of saying, "This book feels too hard for you. Let's make it a 'get to' book, or else finish it up quickly, and get into books that will go faster for you, or "This book feels easy for you. Let's make this series 'weekend reading' and find some books that will match your capabilities as a reader. You need more of a challenge."

There will also be the kids whom you need to coach about fitting more reading into their lives. Sometimes it is simply that kids' lives are . . . complicated, and they need you to be a combination of life coach and cheerleader to help them find more time to read. My final round of conferences or small groups, then, will be with kids who could be moving so much faster as readers if they could get more reading in. I might make appointments with these students, so I can talk with more intimacy. A student and I might call a parent or guardian so that together, we can think how we can give more support to this reader. I might set up a schedule of pages to read over the next few days, and times when I can text them. I might call home and ask for extra support. I might enlist a reading buddy. I might suggest they come early or stay late or come up at lunch, and read in my classroom. Mostly, I want them to know I am on their side, and I am not going away, and that we will keep working on this together.

For your share, you might invite students to apply lessons learned from studying characters to get insights into real people in their own lives. Channel students to be more insightful in how they see people, based on what they learned from thinking deeply about characters. You might point to your anchor chart and say, "Readers, you've been on a deep study of characters' traits. This work will also pay off in your own life—in how you see yourself and others. If you were to make a personal resolution, to be more insightful and generous in how you see the real people in your life, which of these strategies might help you? Are you hard on yourself, or on others? Might you vow to consider the pressures on other people, or on you? Do you tend to hold onto opinions about people forever? Might you vow to look for how people have changed?" Invite students to make a resolution about their own character and to share with a partner.

For homework, you might suggest that readers look back over the reading, thinking, and writing they have done and write an entry about what they have learned so far in this unit—what new reading strengths they have, what new insights into characters in books and people in their life?

Well done!
Mary

FIG. 8–1 Chloe's notebook is an examplar. Here, she reflects on her reading life and makes plans for what's next.

BEND II Investigating How Setting Shapes Characters

A Letter to Teachers

Dear Teachers,

Settings matter. Many teens read, not really noticing or thinking about where the story takes place, or when, or how the specifics of that time and place might shape characters. Yet settings matter tremendously in the kinds of novels they are reading, and in the increasingly complex ones they will begin to read soon.

In this bend of the unit you'll bring students along on a deep investigation of the role that setting plays in shaping characters, in the stories they are reading and the lives they are living. You'll begin the bend with a read-aloud of Adam Bagdasarian's "The Fight," from *First French Kiss*. Will is four years older now than he was in "Popularity," and his middle school is rougher than the elementary school yard where he had jostled for position using words. The setting seems entirely mundane—the whole story happens over two days in eighth grade, at school. Yet, as in so many realistic fiction novels your students are reading, it's a certain kind of school, with its own atmosphere that shapes what happens and doesn't happen there. You'll teach students to investigate this atmosphere, to figure out how the psychology of the place affects characters' choices, and how the author's specific language develops the setting.

Across this bend you'll not only teach students to consider the psychological setting and how it shapes characters, you'll investigate how settings change across a story (even if the location remains the same), how settings affect different characters differently, and how characters can shape settings as well as be shaped by them. You'll also think about time changes as part of changes in setting, so that you can alert students to how authors often use time shifts to bring in backstory. Throughout all of this work on setting, the focus will remain on studying characters and how they interact with other story elements.

It would have been easier, in some ways, in the read-aloud, to study setting in a historical fiction or fantasy story, but I suggest another Bagdasarian story for a few reasons. One is to focus on the mood of the setting rather than its physical or historical characteristics. Another reason is to study the places a character inhabits over time. You can simulate the work of investigating places and characters over a novel, by moving across related short stories. You'll see that you return to moments from "Popularity," comparing the setting and the protagonist across these stories.

If you are also teaching writing workshop, you can call on the work you do here with setting, to think in fiction or personal narrative about how the challenges (physical and emotional) of a place help shape characters. It's a great gift for young writers to realize that trouble is the friend of the writer, and that places that are full of challenge tend to produce complex, compassionate, resilient characters, in books and in the world. If your students are writing literary essays rather than narratives, they may find it interesting to explore how the setting in their stories shapes their characters. Students will continue to be doing a lot of short writing about reading in this bend, and will begin to do some longer writing.

This bend of the unit moves students toward increased independence, toward thinking and talking across books, and toward analyzing the complex interactions of characters and setting. Partnerships continue to be a cornerstone of students' work, as do courses of study. Right now, these courses are really just a few books that go together. The aim is to get students thinking about what books will take them forward, not simply entertain them. For some readers—those who are especially high-level readers and those who read below grade level—getting them on courses of study that map out their reading lives can make a significant difference in their movement. With high-level readers, make sure they choose books of increased complexity, while being wary of content that feels wildly inappropriate for their age. With readers who read below grade level, if you can deliberately get them into series at the upper edge of their comprehension level, and then have the next series in line that's one level up, they'll move faster.

In the last session of Bend I, you thought about shifting partnerships that weren't working and helping students renegotiate book choices that seemed too hard or too easy. As in Bend I, if you have multiple copies of books, encourage partners to read the same books so that they have more to say to each other. Partners will also have more to say to each other if they are swapping books or reading in the same series, same genre, or same author. It's also possible, if your students become good at seeking books through libraries, used copies, and bookstores, that some partnerships might combine to form small clubs.

By now, many of your students should be beginning their third book, with some avid readers (and readers who read considerably below grade level) reading their fourth or fifth book. Keep an eye on reading volume, and more importantly, help students keep an eye on their own reading volume. If volume begins to drop instead of increasing, investigate if a student has gotten into books that are too hard, or if something has changed that is getting in the way of reading.

You'll want to choose the books you talk about and carry with you. Every time you bring in a book that you are reading for pleasure, you model what it means to fit reading into your life. Every time you talk about staying up late reading, or getting a book recommendation from a student and trying it, you help kids envision the life of a reader. As you prepare for this bend, look over the minilessons, rehearse your read-aloud, and think about how you can keep instilling an image of reading beyond the boundaries of the school day. Oscar Wilde wrote, "It is what you read when you don't have to that determines what you will be when you can't help it." Part of our work is to get kids to *want* to read when they don't have to.

All the best,
Mary

Read-Aloud

Characters Are Often Shaped by the Mood or Atmosphere of the Setting

GETTING READY

- ✓ Choose your read-aloud for Bend II (we read the first half of "The Fight" by Adam Bagdasarian, from *First French Kiss*). Prepare to teach by noting places in the text where you will demonstrate a strategy and where you'll prompt kids to practice that strategy with your support. Jot ideas for anticipated coaching.
- ✓ Ask students to bring their homework to discuss at beginning of class (see Connection).
- ✓ Refer to Bend I anchor chart, "To Think Deeply about Characters." You may provide mini-copies that students can tuck into their notebooks (see Connection and Conducting the Read-Aloud).
- ✓ Convene students for the read-aloud, each with a partner, a reading notebook, and their own book (see Link, Independent Reading, and Share).
- ✓ Prepare to listen to partner talk. Students may *not* yet be doing the work the feedback aims to support, but if they are, be prepared to name and compliment that work, encouraging them to do more of it (see Conducting the Read-Aloud).
- ✓ Have large sticky notes on hand to jot students' words to describe mood in the story (see Conducting the Read-Aloud).
- ✓ Display Bend II anchor chart, "To Investigate the Influence of Setting on Characters . . ." (see Conducting the Read-Aloud).

IN THIS SESSION

TODAY YOU'LL use your read-aloud of the first half of "The Fight" by Adam Bagdasarian to teach students that even when the setting is the sort they are apt to overlook because it seems ordinary, it can affect characters deeply. You'll highlight the importance of a setting's mood.

TODAY YOUR STUDENTS will spend most of their time listening, talking, and jotting about the read-aloud, although they'll also have a few minutes at the end of the workshop to continue reading their self-selected books based on the course of study they've taken on with their partner. As they are probably well into their second or third book in their courses of study, and they probably started with easier books, some may have moved up a level of text complexity.

CONNECTION

Recall the work of Bend I and the reflections students wrote last night for homework. Give students a chance to share with each other.

"Readers, this past week and a half, you've been moving into ever-more sophisticated terrain with character traits, and with taking charge of your own reading life." I pointed to our Bend I anchor chart. "Last night, you wrote long about what you've learned, what you're stronger at, since the unit began. Will you get that writing out now and discuss it with your partner? What do you feel you're stronger at? How have you grown as a reader and a thinker?"

I listened to students talk, and then gathered their attention again.

"Readers, I love hearing how you're becoming more powerful readers and thinkers. Some of you said one way you've grown is that you expect characters to be more complicated. Some said you expect to get to know characters more slowly. A few of you talked about seeing different sides of characters, including the pressures that are on them, or reasons they do unlikeable things. Others talked about trying to fit more reading in, or making your writing about reading more powerful.

"Going forward, you want to keep doing this work, whenever you are reading, and you want to layer new work on top. Reading is like a sport—the better you get, the more moves you can make in the game."

Channel kids to listen, attentive to details that suggest *what kind of* place this is.

"Today I want to invite you to do something that powerful readers do—to investigate the impact of settings on characters. To do this work, you'll consider not just the physical characteristics of setting, where it takes place and when, but also its mood or atmosphere.

"In our read-aloud today, let's try out this thinking work. Here's a tip. When the setting seems ordinary, like it's 'just a school,' you have to think extra hard. Some readers would say the setting is 'just middle school,' thinking the setting doesn't really matter. But you'll be the kind of readers who asks, *what kind of* school? Is it the *kind of school* where kids are good to each other? Or is it a place where kids can be cruel or hurtful? Because when you ask those kinds of questions, you'll develop theories about how the mood or atmosphere of this particular place shapes the characters.

"Ready? We're going to read another story about Will, from *First French Kiss*. He's a little older in this story. Last time, he was in fourth grade. In this story, Will is in eighth grade.

"Let's start reading, and as we do, let's ponder what kind of place this is. We might also consider the other reading work the story wants us to be doing now. Even though we're shifting focus to setting, we'll probably want to draw on some of the character work we did earlier as we get to know this older Will."

I looked at what students had brought and added, "I love that you brought your notebook and some Post-its. If for some reason you weren't thinking of that, grab them now, quickly! By now you know that you always want something to write with when you read."

You'll see that this bend of the unit and this session move students to analyze the mood or atmosphere of a place and how that affects characters. You'll also want to remind students that, at the start of a new story, sometimes the story demands some thinking about character traits as well. The truth is, readers do a lot of reading work simultaneously. We isolate strategies to help students hone their skills, but we also want to acknowledge this tension.

CONDUCTING THE READ-ALOUD

Read the beginning of the story, using your voice and gestures to exaggerate the drama in the scene.

> ### The Fight
>
> It began with a basketball game. Mike Dichter and I went up for the same rebound, and I accidentally stuck my elbow in his chest. Then Mike stuck his elbow in my chest, pointed a finger at me, and told me to watch out. In those days I had a reputation for toughness to maintain, so I told him that *he* better watch out, and on the next rebound neither of us watched out and both of us got elbows in the chest. Then we started shoving each other under the basket and pointing fingers and making threatening faces, which was fine with me because looking threatening was one of the things I did best.
>
> Before things could get out of hand, however, gym ended, and Mike and I glared at each other and went back to our respective homerooms.

Invite partners to do the intellectual work that the story seems to call for, requiring them to draw on all they have already learned about thinking about character traits.

"The story is calling for us to think about character traits, isn't it? That'll be true at the start of most stories, when the big job for readers is to get to know the characters. The good thing is you know a lot about ways to think about characters. Look back at our anchor chart if you need ideas. Go ahead, tell your partner what you're thinking so far."

I listened in as partners discussed Will's posing and desire to impress his peers. Then I called them back.

"It's four years later, and Will seems to still have issues with wanting to be cool. Now it's almost worse—he wants to dominate, not just be accepted. Maybe hanging with the cool kids has gone to his head!"

Reread the same excerpt, focusing students' thinking now on the mood or atmosphere of the setting.

"One thing we're realizing is that we don't *stop* doing character trait work when we take on a new lens. Thinking about characters can become something you do almost automatically, like thinking about the people in your life. And *then*, you can push yourself to think about some new aspects of a story.

"Let's reread that part, now that we know what happens, and how pushy Will is. Only this time, let's read with the lens of setting. Ask yourself: 'What *kind* of gym class is this? What's the *mood*? Is it lighthearted? Is it something else?' I'll think about it as well, and we can compare our thinking."

I reread the same excerpt of the story.

Here, you shift lenses, to lead students into new thinking work. You also narrow their gaze, creating a lens that focuses readers on the mood of the setting.

Give students a moment to ponder, then demonstrate how you think about the mood. Invite students to compare their thinking.

"Think now. What words would you use to describe this gym class? Just as you did at the start of this unit when you were first thinking about your characters' traits, try to reach for exactly the right words, and jot those down." I waited a moment. "So let's compare. I'm thinking . . . *nasty*. The mood doesn't seem lighthearted or playful. It feels like something else, with . . ." I looked back at the text. "All those actions—elbows being stuck in chests, finger pointing, being told to 'watch out'—feel kind of mean to me, kind of nasty and unsportsmanlike.

"What do you think? What words did you jot down to describe the mood here? Tell your partner."

I listened in, then called students back to summarize. "I heard many of you weighing options to come up with exactly the right words. One partnership first said the atmosphere is *pushy*, but then refined their thinking and said *competitive*. Some noticed *bullying*. I heard others of you discuss options and land at *intimidating*, which fits all the elbows and finger pointing and shoving. A couple of you said *fake*, wondering if it's not real violence, at least not yet." I jotted a few ideas on large sticky notes to record students' thinking.

Gym Class at Will's School

Nasty | Competitive | Intimidating

You can insert the names of your students to give students props and develop their academic capital by saying, "I heard Juan say . . ." and "I heard Sarah and Maysoon say. . . ." Alfred Tatum and Pedro Noguera both suggest that it's important to role-play kids into the academic identities you want for them. Summarizing (and slightly elevating) kids' discourse is a stop in this role-playing toward academic identities.

"It makes me wonder if Will's whole school is always like this, or if gym class is especially nasty."

Engage students in questioning how the mood in place might shape the character. Set them up to look for details that might help you answer this question, and then read on in the text.

"Readers, you've done some nice work now, thinking about the text with the lens of setting. So many readers would have just said, 'It's just gym class, there's no real setting.' But you reread, thinking about the mood, or atmosphere of this place, and it turns out, it's kind of awful.

"Let's investigate how this mood—nasty-competitive-intimidating-fake—might shape the character. I'm guessing that Will's actions and decisions will be affected by this atmosphere. Let's read on and try to figure out how this place might wrap around Will, exerting pressure to be nasty-mean-competitive-intimidating-fake."

Read on, then invite readers to turn and talk, letting them first talk about what is happening in the story, and then what they're noticing about Will.

> Before things could get out of hand, however, gym ended, and Mike and I glared at each other and went back to our respective homerooms.
>
> Things probably would have taken a peaceful turn if I hadn't walked home with Kevin Cox after school and told him that the next time Mike and I played basketball I was really going to throw some elbows, and if he, Mike, didn't like it, I would fight him anytime, anywhere. I don't know why I said this. Perhaps I was thinking of the Mike I had known a year before. Perhaps I was thinking of the thin, gullible, good-natured Mike who had since grown four inches, gained fifteen pounds, and become as humorless and menacing as a drill sergeant.
>
> Kevin looked at me doubtfully.
>
> "Do you really think you can take him?" he asked me.
>
> Since Kevin had always been one of my most loyal and servile followers, I was astonished by his doubt in my physical prowess.
>
> "I know I can take him," I said.
>
> "He's three inches taller than you," Kevin said.
>
> "So?"
>
> "He's really strong."
>
> "I'm really strong."
>
> Kevin shrugged. "Okay," he said, "but I think Mike could take you."
>
> Now it was my turn to shrug. It was also my turn to lay a condescending hand upon Kevin's shoulder and leave him to ponder his absurd and traitorous notions.
>
> The next day in school everything proceeded as usual. I listened to the teachers, took notes, fell asleep, made a few uncalled-for remarks, and gazed at Denise Young's legs.
>
> During lunch I was sitting with a tableful of friends, talking and listening in my usual superior way, when I heard Mike Dichter say, "Hey, buddy!" Somehow I knew that he meant me. Somehow I also knew that all kinds of jigs were up and that something momentous was going to happen. I turned to look at him.
>
> "I hear you want to fight me," he said.
>
> "That's right," I said.
>
> "I'll meet you after school."
>
> "I'll be there," I said. Then he walked away, and I discovered two interesting things about myself. The first was that the idea of fighting terrified me, and the second was that in moments of extreme fear my body produced ice-cold sweat.
>
> Someone said something to me, and I smiled and nodded. Someone said something else to me, and I smiled and nodded at that too. Perhaps they were giving me advice. Perhaps they were telling me to stay low and lead with my left. I stood up, without really knowing I was standing up, and walked from the cafeteria to the playground. I had never felt so lonely or so frightened in my life. Somehow I had taken a wrong turn and wound up in the wrong day, in the wrong body, with the wrong future. Somehow, in three hours, I was going to be in a real fight with real fists, and there was no way out of it.

"Readers, I'm sure you want to talk about what's happening." I made a frustrated face. "Why does Will have to be so foolish and superior? Talk to your partner." I gave them a minute to talk about the plot, the place, and Will's actions and traits.

Debrief what you heard students say. Set students up to listen to the excerpt again, this time with the lens of setting.

"Readers, I hear you thinking about how snotty Will can be and how he's going to get himself into trouble. I'm with you. Let's also push ourselves to do the new work we're trying to take on in this bend, and think, 'How might the setting be affecting the character?'

"In a moment, let's continue with that lens, but first, let's consider what we know about the setting and how it's shaping Will. Usually when we study a place, we consider the season, or the time period, or the city where it takes place—but the setting is more than that. It's also the mood, or atmosphere, of a place. The way a place shapes a person is often about the way it *feels*.

"I'm thinking of the last story and this one, and how school has changed. Hmm, . . . in the first story, Will was in elementary school and his school, or at least the yard at recess, was kind of intimidating. Being with the cool kids meant playing tag, making jokes on the playground. Now he's in middle school—in *eighth grade*. Gym class, anyhow, has become threatening. Being with the cool kids is very different now. So the setting, even though it's Will's school in both stories, has changed.

"So we have the biggest changes in the setting in mind. Let's reread, noticing details of how this place has changed. Let's ask ourselves, 'What kind of place is this? How might it be affecting Will?'"

Reread, emphasizing parts that suggest setting details.

I reread from the lunch scene until the end of the section, using my voice to emphasize lines such as "superior," "jigs were up," and "real fight, with real fists."

> During lunch I was sitting with a tableful of friends, talking and listening in my usual superior way, when I heard Mike Dichter say, "Hey, buddy!" Somehow I knew that he meant me. Somehow I also knew that all kinds of jigs were up and that something momentous was going to happen. I turned to look at him.
>
> "I hear you want to fight me," he said.
>
> "That's right," I said.
>
> "I'll meet you after school."
>
> "I'll be there," I said. Then he walked away, and I discovered two interesting things about myself. The first was that the idea of fighting terrified me, and the second was that in moments of extreme fear my body produced ice-cold sweat.
>
> Someone said something to me, and I smiled and nodded. Someone said something else to me, and I smiled and nodded at that too. Perhaps they were giving me advice. Perhaps they were telling me to stay low and lead with my left. I stood up, without really knowing I was standing up, and walked from the cafeteria to the playground. I had never felt so lonely or so frightened in my life. Somehow I had taken a wrong turn and wound up in the wrong day, in the wrong body, with the wrong future. Somehow, in three hours, I was going to be in a real fight with real fists, and there was no way out of it.

Set up a partner share. Then think aloud, demonstrating how you think back to the story's start, accumulating details about the setting and its effect on the character.

"Go ahead, share with a partner. I'll give you some help if you feel a little stuck. It's tricky, figuring out what kind of school this is, and how it might shape Will."

I coached students as they talked, directing them to language Will uses that suggests what kind of place his school is. To one partnership, I said, "What do you think Will means when he says, 'All kinds of jigs were up?' Maybe like he's about to get found out? What does that suggest about this place and how Will must act to fit in?"

After giving students a minute to talk, I interrupted.

"Readers, I see you noticing clues in the story about how the setting influences characters. I hear you saying that students like Mike have changed dramatically, becoming big and tough. Some said that Will seems to sit with a bunch of friends in the cafeteria being superior—and you noted that nobody speaks up to say something like, 'Fighting over a gym class is ridiculous,' when Mike calls Will out in the cafeteria.

"The next step is to put these clues together to analyze how setting affects the whole story. First, I might think about all the details, including those from the beginning." I pointed to our chart describing Will's gym class. "All those details showed gym class was a nasty, intimidating place. Now I'm adding in that the kids have become bigger and tougher. The cafeteria seems like a place where kids are posing. Will is acting superior, Mike is acting tough, and all the other kids seem to be just . . . watching.

"All those details make me think two things. This school is a place where it's important to be tough, and it's a place where what you show on the outside matters more than what you feel on the inside. Everyone seems to be acting. And Will fits right in. It's like he wants to fit into this place, and this is a *tough* place."

I paused, noting nods, and scanning for looks of confusion, as well.

"See what I did? I gathered the details, from the beginning of the story, and thought about the kind of atmosphere of this place. Then I thought about what's important in this place, what matters most to the kids. I realized it's important to seem tough. When I think about how this place shapes Will, it begins to make sense. He needs to be tough, because that's what matters in this place."

Read on, inviting students to confirm or expand the theories you have developed together.

"As we read a bit more, see if this part suggests new thinking about this place, or if it confirms that it is a tough place, and that it's making Will need to be tough, even if he may not feel that way." I read aloud.

> My biggest problem, I knew, was that I didn't hate Mike or even dislike him. I had no animal rage to ball my hands into fists and thrust them into action—no deep-seated envy or resentment to impel me toward him with the object of destruction. All I had was fear and pride, which is a pretty poor combination as far as fighting is concerned, because all pride could do was guarantee that I show up for the fight, and all fear could do was guarantee that I lose it.

> The rest of the day passed in a haze of anticipation and dread. I sat through my classes, a smiling silent shell of my former self, and tried to look as casual and confident as possible. Now and then I would look up at the clock and realize that the fight was only one hour and forty-nine minutes away—one hour and forty minutes . . . I tried to tell myself that it might only be a one- or two-punch fight, that maybe Mike would throw a punch and I would throw a punch and we would both smile, throw our arms around each other, and become friends for life. But I knew that it would not be a one- or two-punch fight. No. It would be a fight to some extreme and horrifying limit—a fight to unconsciousness or hospitalization or reconstructive surgery.

"Unconsciousness or hospitalization! Partners, what are you thinking about our theories about this place being pretty tough? What does that mean for Will?!" I gave them a moment to talk.

Summarize the thinking work you've done together, and reveal a new anchor chart for this bend.

"I heard you say that Will's words seem to confirm that this place is tough. He expects this fight to be serious. Our theory about this place seems confirmed. Will is going to have to be pretty tough to survive.

"I know, I want to read on, too! For now, let's name some of the reading work we did, since it's interesting, tricky work. First, all the work that you've learned to do, thinking about character, continues to be critical, particularly at the start of a story," and I gestured to the anchor chart from Bend I. "You'll definitely want to continue thinking and jotting about characters as you read.

"You also found it can pay off when you're studying characters to investigate the setting—especially its mood— as it may influence and shape the character. I started a chart to capture this new work, so you can go on with it in your books." Revealing the chart, I pointed to each bullet as I spoke.

"Investigating setting begins with asking, 'What kind of place is this?' even if the place at first seems ordinary. Then we might consider the mood of the place, which would include thinking about the atmosphere and the ways that people treat each other there."

With Smart Boards common in so many middle school classrooms, it can be easy to no longer have any record in the room of what you've taught. Anchor charts, whether they are large or small, handwritten or printed as mini-charts, help kids remember and refer to the strategies they've been taught. They serve as a guide to students to remind them of the thinking work they should be trying.

ANCHOR CHART

To Investigate the Influence of Setting on Characters . . .

- **Ask, "What kind of place is this?"**
- **Consider the mood of the place.**
  - **the atmosphere**
  - **how people treat each other**

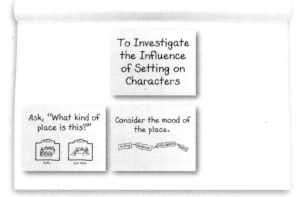

SESSION 9: READ-ALOUD

LINK

Invite students to carry this thinking into their own books. Send them off for a brief time to read.

"This setting work isn't thinking you can just do in 'The Fight.' Will isn't the *only* character who is affected by his setting, and this school isn't the *only* place that has its own kind of mood or atmosphere. Some of you are reading *The Hunger Games*. The Arena definitely has its own atmosphere or if you're reading *The Fault in Our Stars*, I wonder what the mood might be like in a home of a family struggling with a cancer diagnosis? How might the mood affect the character?

"I'll be curious what words you think of to describe the atmosphere or mood of your settings, and how you think these places are affecting your characters. In the time we have, will you reread with this lens? Think for a minute about parts you'll go back and reread, parts where you think this new work will especially pay off. You probably already know what the setting is, when and where the story takes place. Find spots where you can push your thinking about how the setting affects the characters further. Those of you starting a new book might read the beginning twice with this lens in mind. Do you have a plan? Then off you go!"

INDEPENDENT READING

Supporting Students to Reread to Start Analyzing Settings in Their Own Books

Today, readers will continue reading their books from the last bend. If they finish, they will choose a new novel from the library related to their course of study. It isn't necessary to reorganize the classroom library to prioritize books with rich settings, as the goal is for students to practice this setting work even when settings seem familiar.

Because the read-aloud is longer than a minilesson, you may only have time for quick check-ins, probably with groups of students at tables or clusters. You may want to begin with a rapid sweep to make sure students are moving along in their reading and are near finishing their second book, at least.

In the link, you rallied kids to reread select chapters of their books to begin analyzing the setting. It is important that you really believe in the value of rereading. We think we haven't championed this enough. You definitely will want to talk up the value of rereading. You might find students need support identifying parts of their books where this work would particularly pay off. You might voice over comments to the whole class or specific groups such as, "I see a few of you rereading the beginning of the book. That's often where the setting is first introduced and you'll get the first clues as to the mood, the atmosphere, of the place." "Some of you are rereading the major point of conflict. Often the setting is significant there." Give brief, encouraging comments to get all kids going on this line of work.

SHARE

Invite readers to share some of their initial thinking about setting with each other.

Near the end of class, I said, "Readers, take a minute to share some of your thinking with each other. Name three or four phrases you've come up with to describe the setting in your books—the kind of place and what its mood seems to be. You might do some comparing with the book you read just before this, as well. When you explain your thinking, tell each other what details helped you to formulate those ideas."

SESSION 9 HOMEWORK

READ AND THINK: HOW DOES SETTING AFFECT CHARACTER?

Tonight, aim to read for at least thirty to forty minutes, and most importantly, to read twenty-five to forty pages, no matter how long it takes! Some of you will read a lot more than that. Take one second to record your reading so you'll be able to keep track of it.

As you read, if you find yourself doing character work (traits) and setting work, use different-color Post-its, so that your thinking about characters that stems from last week's work is on one color Post-it, and new thinking about setting is on a different color. And will you note two places in your book where the setting seems particularly significant? Flag those places, so you're ready to share them with your partner. Then use your notebook to do a little thinking about them. You might create a two-column chart or a timeline, with one side describing the mood or atmosphere of the setting and the other side describing how it affects the characters. Or you might figure out another way to think about the setting. Perhaps you'll sketch the setting and label your sketch with words that capture the shifting mood. Maybe you'll want to record phrases that reveal the setting, and write about the decisions the author made to use those specific words. Do whatever you decide—but think about the specific passages you select as important.

Session 10

Readers Attend to the Precise Language Authors Use to Describe the Setting

GETTING READY

- Prepare to read aloud and display a brief section from the read-aloud text, "Popularity" (see Teaching).
- Students need their books, notebooks, and homework (see Connection and Active Engagement).
- Display and add to Bend II anchor chart, "To Investigate the Influence of Setting on Characters" (see Link).
- You may want to give some students one or both of these tools, "To Go from Talking to Citing Text" and/or "To Go from Citing the Text to Discussing What You Think" (see Conferring and Small-Group Work).
- Provide copies of the tool, "To Go from Citing the Text to Discussing What You Think," to each student (see Share and Homework).

IN THIS SESSION

TODAY YOU'LL teach your students that when readers think about how the setting influences characters, they pay attention to the author's specific language. This helps readers to grasp the mood, atmosphere, norms, and tempo of a place—all of which can matter in deep and hidden ways to a character.

TODAY YOUR STUDENTS will continue to read along the sequence of texts they've decided to pursue. They will begin by taking a few minutes to return to places in their novels that they had flagged as important passages for setting and study the author's language, thinking about how specific language evokes emotions and images. They'll lift the level of their writing about reading by citing their texts where appropriate.

MINILESSON

CONNECTION

Invite readers to share their jotting and thinking about setting they did for homework.

"Readers, I'm glad to see that many of you have Post-its in two different colors in the pages of your books that you read last night. Will you share one of the places in your book in which the setting seemed especially significant? Before you do, take a second to find where you jotted some things that you noticed, then go ahead and share."

I listened, and after a few minutes, intervened. "Readers, eyes up here. I want to give you some feedback on the work you're doing." I waited until I had their full attention. "What I noticed just now is that many of you talked about the setting by using just your own words, not using any of the author's words. The story says, 'Icicles hung three feet or more from the eaves, and snow blanketed everything,' and you might have talked about the setting to your partner by saying, 'It was winter, tons of snow.'"

❖ **Name the teaching point.**

"Readers, today I want to teach you that when you think about the setting, it is helpful to pay attention to the author's specific language. This helps you grasp the mood, atmosphere, norms, tempo of the place. Those things can matter in deep and hidden ways to a character."

TEACHING

Demonstrate how you return to passages where the setting seemed important, and you study the specific language, thinking about its literal and figurative meaning.

"Readers, it's worth it to go back to passages where you thought the setting was important, and to note the author's exact words. You might even underline key images, copy powerful phrases into your notebook, and read phrases out loud. For example, in the story I was reading, the fact that the icicles that hang from eaves are three feet or more—that detail matters. Those icicles feel treacherous; they make the winter feel harsh, and isolating, too.

"Watch me do this work. I'm going to go back to 'Popularity,' because when we read that story, I wasn't thinking about the setting so much. This is the part where Will is in the playground, wishing he could be with the popular boys. Listen to this." I read aloud and then displayed part of the story.

> *While the two Allans faced off, I looked across the tar and asphalt . . .*

I underlined the words *tar* and *asphalt* and read them aloud again. "Doesn't 'tar and asphalt' sound kind of grim? It's like this black expanse that separates Will from the other kids. Now that we're thinking about setting, I realize how these words seem to emphasize a sense of darkness. It's not like it said, 'I looked across the green grass and blooming flowers. The sun was shining brightly with a warm glow.' That would have seemed hopeful. But instead, Bagdasarian chose to use the words *tar and asphalt*. A dark, sticky, hot mess."

Demonstrate how you let your study of setting details lead you to insights about the character.

"The next step is to think about what this might mean for the character, Will, and what we can possibly learn about him from the kind of setting he's in. So literally, the setting is dark and sticky, and figuratively, it's a dark, sticky place for Will. He might feel stuck in this place, or hardened to it, like the asphalt seems to suggest."

What you are introducing, here, is the connotative meaning of language, particularly figurative language. You could introduce those academic terms here. I think, though, that it might mean more to students if first they study language (in the read-aloud text in their books), looking for phrases and descriptions that seem to mean more than they say—that are evocative. Then, when they have some examples in mind, you might explain the term connotative. *I could also imagine introducing poetry to demonstrate this point.*

Debrief in ways that highlight the transferability of what you are teaching.

"See how I returned to the text and reread a part I thought was important to the setting, looking for specific words that could be meaningful? Then, see how I thought about what those words conveyed? Next, I considered what insights this might give me about the character's relationship to this place. Readers, I remember thinking that Will seemed trapped in this place. It seemed like the mood was pretty grim, but it wasn't until I looked back at the actual words that I see that the author chose specific words to create that feeling. You can do this work, too. You can look back at specific passages you marked, and see if the author used particular language that we call *figurative* or *suggestive* or *evocative*—it evokes an image, a feeling, or mood."

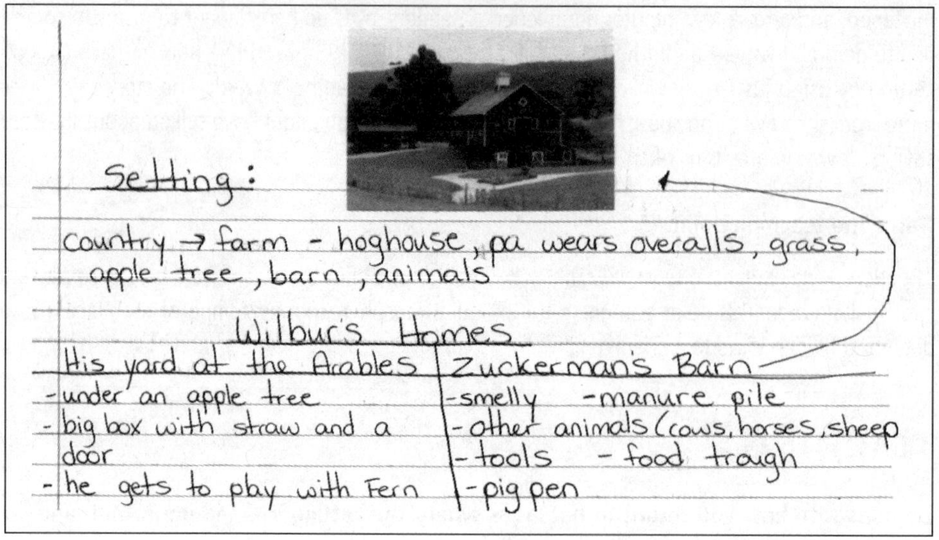

ACTIVE ENGAGEMENT

Prompt students to return to the places in their books that they had flagged as important setting passages, and have them study the precise language the author used.

"You get a chance to try this out now. Take a moment and flip back to a place you marked last night in your book. Study the language. When you have some words or phrases that seem suggestive or evocative, read them aloud to your partner, then talk about why those specific words seem to matter."

I listened as readers found words that described places like the Arena in *The Hunger Games*, the lair of Dauntless in *Divergent*, the Paris restaurant in *The Fault in Our Stars*.

Give students some tips to help them analyze setting details.

"Readers, listening to you, I want to share that some of you are doing similar work. For instance, some are reading aloud words to describe the weather and the season. Here's a tip. Weather is rarely accidental in a story. It's almost always symbolic. You'll see rays of sunshine when things become hopeful, and dark storm clouds when things feel dark, for instance.

"Another tip. Just as I suggested Bagdasarian *could have* written about the green grass and blooming flowers, but instead described the tar and asphalt, I also hear some kids saying, 'He didn't say . . .' or 'She didn't write . . .' That's a great way to investigate language—think about other ways the author could have said something, and then theorize about the impact of the words he or she *did* choose.

FIG. 10–1 Some middle school readers like to download images to help them visualize unfamiliar settings.

"What you're doing, readers, is attending to what's called *connotative language*. It means words that are symbolic or evocative—they evoke an emotional response or call to mind an image. Like 'tar and asphalt' called to mind sticky blackness literally, and a kind of feeling of being trapped and hopeless symbolically. The words you are reading aloud now call to mind certain emotions and images.

"As you go forward with this work, will you be more attentive to language in your books? You're reading novels by some of the great authors of your time. You want to attend to their language. One way to notice their word choice is to study the language they use to describe the places in your books."

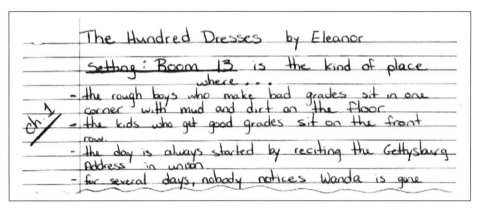

FIG. 10–2 The setting in *100 Dresses* isn't just a school, it's the kind of school where no one notices Wanda is gone.

LINK

Let students know that this work of attending to the author's specific language will support thinking about characters, as well as setting.

"Readers, I'll add this strategy to our teaching chart. Will you be extra alert to language in your books, and note phrases that seem significant—the exact language an author uses? You might flag them or copy them into your notebook. Do this when you are studying setting. It will also pay off when you are doing other thinking work. When you are studying characters, for instance, there will be phrases that are evocative and suggestive, and you'll want to capture them and read them to a partner, and think about them. As you go off today, think about this work as you are reading and jotting."

ANCHOR CHART

To Investigate the Influence of Setting on Characters . . .

- Ask, "What kind of place is this?"
- Consider the mood of the place.
  - the atmosphere
  - how people treat each other
- **Notice how the author's specific language evokes emotions and images.**

Notice how the author's language evokes emotions and images.

SESSION 10: READERS ATTEND TO THE PRECISE LANGUAGE AUTHORS USE TO DESCRIBE THE SETTING

CONFERRING AND SMALL-GROUP WORK

Supporting Students in Citing Texts

AS YOU CONFER AND LEAD SMALL GROUPS, you might consider ways to support students in citing texts in their conversation and their writing about reading.

Help students find specific places in a text, rather than retell whole sections.

Sometime students think they are naming specific passages or parts, and really, they are retelling the plot or the gist of a section. To help students identify the most relevant parts for supporting their thinking, remind them that they are zooming in on the text to look for specific details and encourage them to put their fingers on those lines or place a Post-it next to those lines to frame them. You might push students to determine which words in those lines are most important to supporting their thinking. Ask them, "What specific words in those two lines make you know they are supporting what you are trying to say?"

Offer conversation prompts, or sentence starters, for citing a text specifically.

You might support some students with conversation prompts, or sentence starters, to help them with language for citing a text, whether they are citing specific words to think about setting or about character traits. For example, you might give students a small tool with these phrases on it:

To Go from Talking to Citing the Text:

Early in the book, readers learn, "..."

The author paints the picture, saying, "..."

The text says, "..."

It is (a winter/spring; morning/evening) "..."

(The character) notices, as the story says, "..."

It seems like a _____ place, especially when the author says "..."

You might have one partner point to a sentence starter. Then the other partner needs to try that out, first finding a quick place in the book where he or she can quote the author's specific language. Or, partners together can find a passage to quote, and then try out one of these phrases.

A Deep Study of Character

Offer phrases to help students analyze specific text citations.

For students who find specific parts of the story, but who then need support talking about these parts with more analysis, you might offer some prompts that help students say more. For instance:

> To Go from Citing the Text to Discussing What You Think:
>
> This shows that . . .
>
> This illustrates that . . .
>
> This demonstrates that . . .
>
> Readers realize that . . .
>
> This changes everything. Whereas before . . . now . . .
>
> Readers begin to wonder/question/worry/understand . . .
>
> The important thing to notice about this is that . . .

Watch for students who simply nod or agree with each other when they find passages, and coach them to use these prompts to try to say more—to explain why these phrases or words seem important.

Teach students to lift a line—writing/thinking/talking long from a quote.

Some readers will be struck by certain lines in their novels. You might gather some of these readers, who are often strong readers, and show them the strategy of "lifting a line" and writing/thinking/talking long from it. When readers find a line particularly evocative, they can often write fast and long about it, think long and hard about it, and talk long about it. Often this writing and these conversations lead them to new thinking, as they mull over what it is about a certain line that seems so significant. You might suggest that it can be because something has changed, or because it harkens back to another moment in the novel, and makes that moment more significant. Or some lines are a window into a character or a place, as if it has opened up to the reader. And some authors simply use language in such beautiful and powerful ways that you want to read it aloud, talk about it, remember it.

SHARE

Channeling Partners to Help Each Other Grow Ideas

Ask readers to meet with partners and to share some of their best thinking with one another.

"Readers, at the end of the minilesson today, I suggested you capture evocative or suggestive phrases in your novels to think more deeply about them or share them with a partner. Right now, would you choose a part of your book that felt especially intriguing to share with your partner? When you are the listening partner, it's your job to help your partner to deepen his thinking. Help your partner move from an initial idea to a deeper one, perhaps by prompting him to help him grow his thinking. For example, after your partner shares an intriguing part, you might say, 'The important thing to notice about this is that . . .' and ask him to continue thinking aloud. If it's helpful, refer to the prompts from our 'To Go from Citing the Text to Discussing What You Think' chart to give you ideas. You may take a copy of the chart to use for homework tonight if you'd like."

SESSION 10 HOMEWORK

 PAYING ATTENTION TO SETTING DETAILS

Readers, as you read tonight for your usual thirty to forty minutes, pay special attention when the author is describing the setting. Linger on details that others might pass by, and consider what those details might suggest about the kind of place you are reading about. Choose a few of these setting details to capture in your notebook. You might write a line from your novel, and then spend a few minutes writing long to extend your thinking about it. Use prompts from the "To Go from Citing the Text to Discussing What You Think" chart to help guide your writing, if they're helpful to you.

> To Go from Citing the Text to
> Discussing What You Think:
>
> This shows that . . .
>
> This illustrates that . . .
>
> This demonstrates that . . .
>
> Readers realize that . . .
>
> This changes everything. Whereas before . . . now . . .
>
> Readers begin to wonder/question/worry/understand . . .
>
> The important thing to notice about this is that . . .

Session 11

Sometimes Characters Are Torn by Competing Pressures, Including the Pressures of a Place

IN THIS SESSION

TODAY YOU'LL teach your students that one way to investigate the relationship between the setting and characters is to pay attention to inconsistencies between characters' behaviors and their inner thinking. When characters are torn and inconsistencies arise, it could be that external pressures from their surroundings led them away from their inner compass.

TODAY YOU'LL AIM TO PROVIDE YOUR STUDENTS with a solid half-hour to read today. As they read, their writing about reading and their thinking will probably be influenced by your minilessons highlighting the setting and its effect on characters. If they are far enough along in a new book, they will choose ways of taking notes to investigate when characters seem to act inconsistently.

GETTING READY

- ✓ Display and add to Bend II anchor chart, "To Investigate the Influence of Setting on Characters..." (see Connection and Link).
- ✓ Revisit and display an excerpt from your read-aloud text (see Teaching).
- ✓ Ask students to bring their own books to try this work (see Active Engagement).
- ✓ Display Bend I anchor chart, "To Think Deeply about Characters..." (see Link).
- ✓ Have available some below grade-level books to work with small groups. You may want to create cards with reading work prompts to offer students (see Conferring and Small-Group Work).
- ✓ You may want to print the "Character" strand of the Bands of Text Complexity from *A Guide to the Reading Workshop: Middle School Grades*.

MINILESSON

CONNECTION

Give students a minute to share what they're learning about setting in their novels, based on last night's homework.

"Readers, as you read last night, I bet many of you were thinking of your books in a whole new light, based on the setting work we started yesterday. Would you share your thinking with your partner for a minute? Talk about the key scenes you jotted where the setting felt significant, and share your notes. You can use our anchor chart to guide your conversation. It's also possible that you noticed how the setting is related to the particular kind of book you are reading—the genre, for example."

> **To Investigate the Influence of Setting on Characters...**
>
> - Ask, "What kind of place is this?"
> - Consider the mood of the place.
>   - the atmosphere
>   - how people treat each other
> - Notice how the author's specific language evokes emotions and images.

Remind students of the work you did yesterday, revisiting some of the intricacies of literary language for this work.

"Yesterday we investigated the role that the setting plays in shaping characters.' We thought about the kind of place Will is in, and how the particular mood, or atmosphere of that place, affects him. It's like he's led away from his inner moral compass by the pressures of this place.

"I'm using all those words for a reason. Sometimes when you're reading, it feels like a place has a particular mood that you can give an exact word to—like *grim* or *desolate* or *forbidding*. Other times you just have a sense, that you may not have exact words for, but it's a kind of atmosphere. Maybe things don't feel right, like in a horror movie."

❖ **Name the teaching point.**

"Readers, today I want to teach you that when characters seem torn, when they're acting one way on the outside and a different way on the inside, it's sometimes because they're being pulled in different directions. You can consider ways the pressures of a place might be pulling them away from their inner compass."

TEACHING

Revisit an excerpt from your read-aloud, one that suggests the character is acting in ways that are consistent with the setting but inconsistent with his or her feelings or desires.

"Watch me do this work. I'll bring us back to a part of the story we already read. It's the moment when Mike tracks Will down and says he wants to fight him." I displayed the text and read aloud.

> "I hear you want to fight me," he said.
>
> "That's right," I said.

This reading lesson is another lesson that lends itself to studying the text of one's own life as well as the novels in hand. Do you remember your own middle and high school years, and the pressure (real or imagined) to act in certain ways or dress in certain ways? Don't you wish you could spare our students some of that agony? It's comforting to know that both reading and writing workshop give our students a means of reflecting on these issues—and of realizing they're not alone.

"I'll meet you after school."

"I'll be there," I said. Then he walked away, and I discovered two interesting things about myself. The first was that the idea of fighting terrified me, and the second was that in moments of extreme fear my body produced ice-cold sweat.

Looking at the text, I said, "So, . . . Will *says*, 'That's right,' and 'I'll be there.' He acts on the outside as if he wants to fight Mike. But let's see how he feels inside. Let's study how he reacts in his thoughts. Well, he is thinking that the idea of fighting *terrifies* him. So he feels terrified, but he acts tough.

"Let me think why Will is acting this way. Could it have anything to do with the kind of school he's in? Hmm, . . . based on what we noticed in gym class and the lunchroom, this eighth grade has become a kind of tough place, and that might account for the inconsistency in Will's thoughts and actions. It's the kind of school where you have to be tough and cool, so Will *can't* say, 'Sorry, I don't want to fight you. It was a misunderstanding.' He's torn, right? He has all this inner conflict, but he has to keep a cool exterior. What a mess!"

Recap, taking students through the steps of finding inconsistencies and thinking about the role the setting might play.

"See how I focused on one small moment when a character is torn, where he seems to feel differently on the inside than he acts on the outside? It could be a moment when he thinks one thing and says something else. Or maybe he feels one thing and does something that doesn't jibe with that feeling. I found a moment that showed that inconsistency, asking, how could the pressures of this place account for some of this character's inconsistency?"

ACTIVE ENGAGEMENT

Invite students to try this work in their own books. Channel them to take notes in ways that capture their characters' inconsistencies.

"Readers, I bet a lot of you are reading books where the character may feel torn, pressured, or influenced by the place she finds herself in, and she acts in ways that are contrary to her own desires or moral compass. Like Katniss in the Arena—she doesn't want to kill, but the place won't let her survive if she doesn't. Think of the book you are now reading or a book you've read where these kinds of character inconsistencies might point to the influence of setting. Give me a nod when you've got an idea." I waited.

"Throughout this unit, we've discussed different ways you can take notes to capture your thinking, like T-charts, sketches, or freewriting. Right now, would you set up a page in your notebook to collect some thoughts on these character inconsistencies? You might, for example, create a T-chart with headings like, 'Ways Character Acts Externally' and 'Ways Character Feels Internally' to capture that difference. Or, you might make a sketch that illustrates all of the external pressures acting on your character.

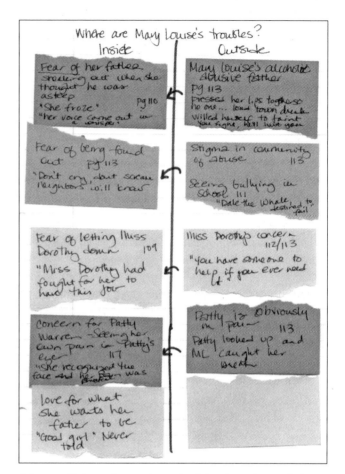

FIG. 11–1 This reader ponders what's inside and outside her character.

• "When you have an idea, get to work."

I gave students a minute to jot, leaning in to study their work as they jotted or sketched about the kinds of pressures exerted in dystopian settings and historical fiction, and the kinds of schools and homes they were finding in realistic fiction, and how those could account for characters acting against their own interests.

LINK

Add this work to students' repertoire, reminding them that they can use the anchor chart to help them set their own reading work. Then send them off.

"Readers, let's add this work to your repertoire—and to the anchor chart. I think it will help you see the influence of the setting on characters in your novels more specifically. Be extra alert if you notice these kinds of character inconsistencies in the next few days, so we can test this theory.

"Remember, you can use this anchor chart, along with our anchor chart from last week, to help you set your own reading work. Be ambitious in two ways. Set yourself enough work to keep you fully engaged for about half an hour. And don't slide into easy, familiar work. Challenge yourself!

"Take a second to tell your partner what work you will do today, and why. When you have a smart plan, off you go."

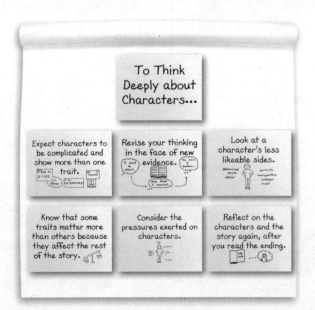

ANCHOR CHART

To Investigate the Influence of Setting on Characters . . .

- Ask, "What kind of place is this?"
- Consider the mood of the place.
  - the atmosphere
  - how people treat each other
- Notice how the author's specific language evokes emotions and images.
- **Ask, "Is a character torn? Is something in the setting pulling a character between competing pressures?"**

Ask, "Is something in the setting pulling a character between competing pressures?"

CONFERRING AND SMALL-GROUP WORK

Using Bands of Text Complexity to Introduce New Reading Work

ONE POWERFUL WAY TO HELP STUDENTS move up levels of complexity is by introducing them to the fascinating challenges of the next level, or band of levels, and sharing tips on negotiating these challenges. You may have some readers who are reading far below benchmark, at level L or M, for example. In your work with these students, guide them toward the next band of text complexity, which starts at level N. In this way, you can help them to do the thinking work that will be required of them at the next level so that they will be more prepared to take on the new level's challenges when they are ready to move up. You can read more about bands of text complexity, and about how helpful it is to know more about reading levels in general, in the *A Guide to Reading Workshop: Middle School Grades*.

You might, for instance, pull some students who are reading around level P–Q to help them move into R–S–T books. You might choose books such as *Because of Winn Dixie*, and *Bridge to Terabithia*, or picture books like *Fly Away Home* and *Freedom Summer*. (If you have access to the TCRWP Classroom Libraries, check the Grade 6 or Grade 7 Below Benchmark shelves for books in this band.)

Pull these students together and tell them you're excited for them to be moving into more complex novels. To inspire readers, you might say, "You'll be reading more sophisticated books next, so your reading has to become more sophisticated, too. I'll help you match what you're doing as a reader to the kinds of books you'll be reading."

Then, you might gather them around a shared book that is the level of text you're supporting them toward. You might create a few cards with prompts highlighting reading work that they can use to challenge themselves as they read more complex novels. They can try out the reading work suggested by each card, focusing on character and setting work, since that is the work of the unit so far. To help with transference, you might offer students a set of these cards related to the band and the unit to push their thinking in their own books.

If you are moving students into U–V books, books such as *Percy Jackson and the Lightning Thief*, you might have a different set of cards related to the band and the unit.

Reading Work Prompts for Levels R-S-T

The setting often becomes specific and unusual . . . and important! Think about how the setting specifically shapes the character.	Characters bump into troubles that are bigger than they are that they can't solve easily. Try to name the troubles that are inside the character and outside. See if some might be social issues.	Problems multiply, and aren't easily solved. Try to name not just the big problem, but the smaller or more secret problems and pressures that characters face.
Minor characters are there for a reason—ask yourself why!	You can learn a lot about characters by how they deal with trouble. See what traits emerge.	The end of the story may not always solve all the character's problems. Try to figure out what does and doesn't change by the end for the character.

SESSION 11: SOMETIMES CHARACTERS ARE TORN BY COMPETING PRESSURES, INCLUDING THE PRESSURES OF A PLACE

Reading Work Prompts for Levels U-V-W

The setting will often change rapidly in a few ways. It might literally change—the characters are in different places. And it might change in its mood—so it becomes a more dangerous or safer place. Try to notice when the setting changes, and *how you know*—the words the author uses.	Characters' strengths and flaws often have a huge impact on the story. Ask yourself about characters' strengths and flaws, and which ones seem to be affecting the plot the most at any given time.	Characters' motivations in any given moment are often shaped by events earlier in the story. See if you can figure out, in moments of critical action or decision, what pressures, needs, or wants might shape a character's decisions.
Time often changes rapidly in these stories. There may be flashbacks, there may be ways the author inserts backstory, there may be sudden shifts forward in time. Try to notice when time changes, and how you know—the cues the author gives you.	Characters in these stories are often not what they seem. See if you notice clues (it might be when rereading) that characters are different than they seemed at first.	Characters' traits will often change across these stories, as characters learn lessons—that is, the lessons aren't only at the end of the book. See if you notice traits that are changing and develop evidence-based theories for why they change.

When you frame the work as new, challenging, and fascinating, kids usually rise to it and want to do it. Be sure to set up some system for returning to these students. They might form an informal book club and share their courses of study, so you can drop in and coach. They might meet in an informal writing-about-reading group to compare their thinking, referring to their reading notebooks.

SHARE

Figuring Out Why Some Parts Are Important to the Whole of the Story

Readers fit parts of the text in with the whole, asking, "Why did the author include this part?"

"Readers, will you take a moment to look over your Post-its or notebook, or to put your finger on one page in your book if you didn't flag it yet, that seems particularly important to the thinking work you are doing right now?" I waited, adding in, "It might be important to the setting, or to the character traits, to whatever you decided to pay extra attention to—find an important passage.

"When you meet with your partner, will you do some thinking about how this part fits with the whole of your novel so far? That is, when readers are struck by a passage, it's often interesting to ask, 'Why did the author include this part? What about it is so important to the story?'"

SESSION 11 HOMEWORK

 ### READING WORK: CHARACTER TRAITS OR SETTING

Tonight, continue reading and logging the amount of reading you do. Aim to read at least thirty to forty pages as always, and keep track of your reading in your reading log. You are probably reading your third or fourth novel by now. Decide if you want to return to character trait work from last week, or if you want to continue to read with the lens of setting. If you choose character trait work, revisit the strategies you learned, and mark places in your book where you gain new insight into important character traits, pressures, or changes. If you choose setting work, mark places in your book where the setting particularly seems to have an impact on characters.

SESSION 11: SOMETIMES CHARACTERS ARE TORN BY COMPETING PRESSURES, INCLUDING THE PRESSURES OF A PLACE

Session 12

Settings Can Change over Time, Not Just Physically, but Psychologically

GETTING READY

- Prepare to show a video clip from *Stranger Things*, the first eight-minute series opener, start at 4:32 mark. A link to the video is available in the online resources (see Connection).
- Revisit and display two excerpts from your read-aloud text (we read from "Popularity" and "The Fight") (see Teaching).
- Display chart, "Ways to Question the Text about Psychological Setting Changes" (see Teaching).
- Display and add to anchor chart, "To Investigate the Influence of Setting on Characters . . ." (see Link). Provide students with mini-copies of this chart (see Homework).
- You may want to pull partners or combine partnerships reading in the same genres to work on settings (see Conferring and Small-Group Work).
- For readers studying fantasy genre, you may want to show them sketches or images of fantasy settings (see Conferring and Small-Group Work).

IN THIS SESSION

TODAY YOU'LL teach your students that the setting in a story can keep changing not just physically, but psychologically. Readers trace the setting over time, investigating how the place changes, and how it affects characters differently in different moments.

TODAY YOUR STUDENTS will continue to read novels, keeping track of their thinking using their Post-its and notebooks, and later talking with partners about some of their insights. You'll especially channel readers to think about how places in stories may change over time.

MINILESSON

CONNECTION

Bring readers into a popular story where the place changes dramatically for the characters. In this instance, call to mind *Stranger Things* and play a video clip.

"Readers, I've been thinking about our character work so far—and how so far we've been analyzing the setting as if it doesn't change. As if the setting in stories is only one way, and it always affects characters in the same way. But I watched something last night that made me think more about this.

"Like a lot of you, and like millions of watchers around the world, I've spent some time obsessing about *Stranger Things*. Last night, I was watching the first episode again. If you don't know the series, it's set in the eighties. It starts with one of the main characters, a middle school kid. He has been playing Dungeons and Dragons with his friends, and now he sets out to bike home. He's clearly biked home a thousand times, never worrying about his safety.

"Here's the thing. Even though every other night, the woods and the neighborhood have felt safe, things feel different this time. Take a look at this clip."

I played the clip of the boys saying good-bye, Will saying that the demi-gorgon in the game "got him," the lights flickering mysteriously, and Will biking alone to his house. An increasingly ominous journey through ordinary territory.

"There's something ominous here, isn't there? The way the lights flicker, the way the streets seem so empty, the way the woods seem suddenly so quiet, the way even his house doesn't seem safe anymore? It's like you're watching and suddenly you realize that a place that seemed safe *isn't* anymore. It's as if the place seemed to change, or the feeling of the place changed, anyhow, even though it was physically the same."

"Which brings me to this—how we can do similar kinds of work inside of our reading, where we investigate the shifting nature of places in our stories?"

❖ **Name the teaching point.**

"Today I want to teach you that readers come to realize that the setting in a story can keep changing, psychologically even if not physically. They trace the setting over time, investigating how the nature of the place shifts, and how these shifts affect characters."

TEACHING

Read aloud an early scene from your character study, in this case, a scene from "Popularity." Demonstrate how you analyze how the character experiences the setting.

"Let's try this together. I'll take us back to a scene from 'Popularity.' It's the moment after Will has destroyed Mitch. Then we'll put *next* to it a moment later in the story, after Mike has destroyed Will. In both moments, Will is in his town, at his school, surrounded by his peers and friends. Let's see if there is any evidence that this same place has changed for Will."

I put up and read aloud the first excerpt, from "Popularity."

> . . . *No one knew because no one noticed—no one had called him for months. But* my *phone rang*. *My weekends were filled with sleep-overs and baseball games and bowling parties and bicycle races and more new friends than I knew what to do with.*

If you haven't watched Stranger Things, *you may want to put down this book and go watch it. It perfectly captures the loyalties and tensions between these kids against a backdrop of eighties nostalgia.*

"To investigate this setting, I'll consider some of our earlier questions when we first analyzed gym class and the cafeteria in 'The Fight.'" I gestured toward our anchor chart. "I'm thinking that in this scene, Will's neighborhood is the kind of place that's so friendly, so full of joy." I pointed to the words as I said, "It's a place filled with sleepovers and baseball games and bicycle races and more new friends than Will knows what to do with. That tells me a lot about the mood of this place and ways people treat each other. Even though Will is a bit suspicious of his new friends, his neighborhood feels great here, like it is wrapping around him, including him."

Read aloud a scene that shows the character at a later time, in this case, a scene from "The Fight." Invite students to share what they notice about the setting.

I read aloud the second excerpt.

> It began with a basketball game. Mike Dichter and I went up for the same rebound, and I accidentally stuck my elbow in his chest. Then Mike stuck his elbow in my chest, pointed a finger at me, and told me to watch out. In those days I had a reputation for toughness to maintain, so I told him that he better watch out, and on the next rebound neither of us watched out and both of us got elbows in the chest. Then we started shoving each other under the basket and pointing fingers and making threatening faces, which was fine with me because looking threatening was one of the things I did best.
>
> Before things could get out of hand, however, gym ended, and Mike and I glared at each other and went back to our respective homerooms.

I invited students to discuss. "What are you thinking here? Tell your partner, what stands out here? How has this place changed? You might draw on our anchor chart as you talk, like I did."

After a moment, I said, "I hear you saying what I'm thinking, too. This place has a much different feeling for Will." I pointed to the text and said, "It's a place of . . . pointing fingers . . . threatening faces . . . glares . . . In the first story, Will's school and neighborhood are places where he played games that we can assume were actually fun, like the baseball games and bowling parties he mentions, and now it's a place where even the games are harsh and violent."

Recap the conclusions you drew with students. Suggest this work is a way readers can always study characters more deeply.

"Readers, what's interesting about this work is that the place hasn't changed much physically. Both stories are set at Will's school. But it's changing in its mood, or atmosphere, for the character, in this case, Will.

The places in each story are so similar, but they feel so different for Will. I'm thinking a reason for this might be that Will himself has changed. It seems that, over time, fitting in and being popular have become more and more important for him. So much so, that he's been more and more willing to act in ways that don't fit with who he really is. During the gym scene in the second story, he's more and more snarky and threatening, to fit in.

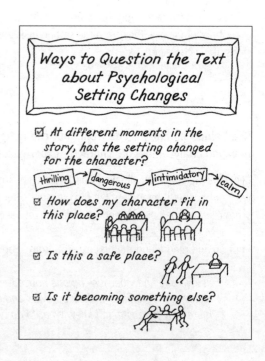

"So as a reader, you question the text, with questions like these." I pointed to the "Ways to Question the Text about Psychological Setting Changes" chart.

ACTIVE ENGAGEMENT

Invite readers to imagine this work in the books they are reading now or in prior books. You might remind students of books they know, or ones that were made into movies that they probably know.

"Readers, let's give you a chance to try this work. Think of a book where the setting feels different at different places in the story. It might be the book you are reading right now, or it might be a book where the setting seems to change dramatically. I'm thinking of books like *Bridge to Terabithia*, or *The Thief of Always*, or *Harry Potter*, or *The Watsons Go to Birmingham*.

"Give me a nod when you've got a book in mind and have a thought about how the setting changes for the character across the story." I waited. "Now compare with your partner. What are you thinking about?"

The kids talked about books where the setting seemed particularly significant, such as *The Thief Lord*, and *The Book Thief*, and *The Maze Runner*.

I listened in to students. When I knew the books, I helped kids push their thinking, saying things like, "You're thinking about *Divergent* . . . so interesting, isn't it, the way Erudite can feel sometimes like a safe place and sometimes like a dangerous place?" or "Isn't it interesting in *The Watsons Go to Birmingham* how the characters change as the places around them change? It's like they are influenced by all of those different places."

After a few minutes, I said, "Readers, you might also try the second part of the work we did, which is use your observations of setting changes to think about ways the characters are changing. Give that a shot."

LINK

Remind students of the work they've been doing, and set them up to add this new thinking to their repertoire.

I called the class back together. "Readers, let's pause in this thinking. I can hear that you're reconsidering books you've read before, as well as reconsidering moments in the books you're reading now, when the way the setting feels for a character begins to change dramatically.

When you mention specific titles that kids have read, or are reading, it personalizes the work for them. Sometimes I'll also say, "Oh, Jordan, this will definitely be interesting in your book," as a way to bring readers into the work.

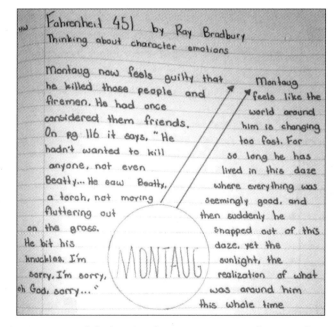

FIG. 12–1 Look for how students return to specific parts of the text in their analyses.

"Add this work to your repertoire of smart ways to think deeply about how the setting in your novels affects the characters. Think about the work you've been doing, decide if you are going to keep on with exactly what you've been doing, or if you're ready to push that thinking further with today's work. Then off you go. I'll add this work to our chart as a reminder."

ANCHOR CHART

To Investigate the Influence of Setting on Characters . . .

- Ask, "What kind of place is this?"
- Consider the mood of the place.
  - the atmosphere
  - how people treat each other
- Notice how the author's specific language evokes emotions and images.
- Ask, "Is a character torn? Is something in the setting pulling a character between competing pressures?"
- **Investigate how the psychology of a place shifts, and how those shifts affect characters.**

Investigate how the psychology of a place shifts, and how those shifts affect characters.

| 6th Grade | 7th Grade | 8th Grade |
| Intimidating | Exciting | Nostalgic |

CONFERRING AND SMALL-GROUP WORK

Genre-Based Small Groups

IN BEND I, you got readers going on courses of study, and you helped them to think about how the character work they plan might be shaped by the particular kinds of books they are reading. Today you might return to that work, thinking with students about how the kinds of books they are reading might shape the ways they think about setting.

Settings in Fantasy Novels

Whether students are reading *Dragon Slayers' Academy* or *Lord of the Rings*, there will be some similarities in the settings in fantasy novels, which is why fantasy readers often love to talk to other fantasy readers. You might pull together your fantasy readers and invite them to think about archetypal settings in their novels. In general, fantasy settings tend to come in three forms. One is the medieval setting, rife with dragons and castles. Another is the modern setting, with fantasy elements that often only appear to some characters. And another is a portal between different lands, and characters can travel from one to the other. Each setting poses different challenges to characters. Your fantasy readers will find it interesting to consider how their novels fit with or break with these archetypal settings, and the particular challenges these settings pose to their characters.

Settings in Historical Fiction Novels

Settings in historical fiction novels tend to develop in a couple of ways. You might explain these to your historical fiction readers, and set them to figure out how their novels fit or break with these patterns. One pattern is that the historical conflict hasn't started yet, or it is just starting, and the character learns about the conflict as the novel develops. In this kind of novel, the reader is on a learning journey alongside the character. Another pattern is that the novel begins in the midst of a historical conflict, and the reader is expected to either know something about this conflict, or to find out. Once students know about these patterns, they might investigate the setting in their novels with these lenses, and consider what pattern their novel fits. Any historical fiction reader would benefit by spending a few minutes on Google images to find photos, maps, and other images of the time period and place of their novel. If students are reading a novel that begins in the midst of conflict, they might use Wikipedia to read briefly about that conflict.

FIG. 12–2   Examples of fantasy settings

Settings in Dystopian Novels

Almost all dystopian novels are set sometime in the future where things have gone awry. Often there is advanced technology, though sometimes things have reverted, after some disaster, to medieval technology, with glimpses of other power. To begin, you might suggest that dystopian readers compare settings, noticing similarities and patterns. Then, in all dystopian novels, a big aspect of the setting is going to be a power hierarchy. It's interesting to ask, "What are the rules here? Who has power?" Chances are, the main character is going to break those rules and subvert that power. If you have some very high-level readers, you can also begin to think about how the settings and issues in dystopian novels mirror real settings and issues, as dystopian novels tend to act as social commentary.

SHARE

Following Up on Courses of Study and Comparing Writing about Reading

Invite readers to study their notes in preparation for talking about their reading.

"Readers, in a few minutes, you'll have some time to share some of the work you are doing in your courses of study in your partnerships. To start, you might show each other the thinking work you've been doing from today and the last few days. To do that, why don't you get your reading notebook ready? Walk through the jotting you've done, and be prepared to give a little tour of your thinking life."

Set students up to talk in partnerships, and to analyze the work their partner is trying. Suggest they draw upon a class chart to lift the level of their feedback.

"Partners, listen up. Really try to analyze how your partner is trying some of the newer, more challenging work we've been studying, and some of the work your genre or author study calls for. Look for how your partner has studied some ideas over pages, over time—or see if instead, you see a kind of 'popcorning' from one idea to a completely different idea. Then, give each other feedback on what you see. Remember to pressure each other in positive ways."

ANCHOR CHART

To Investigate the Influence of Setting on Characters . . .

- Ask, "What kind of place is this?"
- Consider the mood of the place.
  - the atmosphere
  - how people treat each other
- Notice how the author's specific language evokes emotions and images.
- Ask, "Is a character torn? Is something in the setting pulling a character between competing pressures?"
- Investigate how the psychology of a place shifts, and how those shifts affect characters.

SESSION 12 HOMEWORK

 STUDYING YOUR READING WORK

Tonight, just read, read, read, annotating or flagging places where you have an important thought and realize you might want to share this spot with your partner. After you have read, take time to review the places in the book that you have flagged. Think of those places against the anchor chart, asking yourself, "What kind of reading work am I doing independently? How am I challenging myself?"

Then jot a quick entry in your reading notebook, about the reading work you are satisfied with, because the evidence shows you are challenging yourself, and any goals you have for deepening your work. Remember to read at least thirty to forty pages, and to log your reading, as always.

SESSION 12: SETTINGS CAN CHANGE OVER TIME, NOT JUST PHYSICALLY, BUT PSYCHOLOGICALLY

Session 13

Read-Aloud

Characters Acting as a Group Can Wield Enormous Influence, for Good or for Evil

GETTING READY

- Prepare to read aloud the second half of your chosen text for Bend II (we continue reading "The Fight" by Adam Bagdasarian, from *First French Kiss*).
- Students should bring their reading notebooks to the read-aloud.
- Display Bend I anchor chart, "To Think Deeply about Characters" (see Connection).
- Display and add to Bend II anchor chart, "To Investigate the Influence of Setting on Characters . . ." (see Connection, and Link).
- Be ready to show your own notebook pages with headings, "group dynamics," "bad apple," and "good leader" (see Conducting the Read-Aloud).

IN THIS SESSION

TODAY YOU'LL read aloud the second half of your text (we read from "The Fight" from *First French Kiss*). You'll teach students that in addition to places affecting characters, characters can also act as positive or negative forces on a place.

TODAY YOUR STUDENTS will continue reading their self-selected books. They'll do all the work you've highlighted, including thinking deeply about characters and thinking also about the ways the setting influences characters and vice versa. They'll use their reading notebooks to jot notes as they listen, and they'll think about the relationship between the characters and the place.

CONNECTION

Remind students of the intellectual work you've been tackling together, and where you left off in the read-aloud story.

"Readers, we left Will, in 'The Fight,' in a bit of a cliffhanger. Remember, he was thinking about how this fight might lead to unconsciousness, hospitalization, or reconstructive surgery?! That line has haunted me.

"Since we began the story, we've been investigating how the setting—its mood, or atmosphere, or shifting psychology—might influence characters' behaviors. We came to realize that perhaps Will agrees to this fight because, in this school, he can't imagine *not* agreeing. It's like his choices are limited by the place he finds himself in. Can you get your notebooks out, and look over any jottings you made when we started the story, and then can you talk to your partner for a moment, reminding each other both of what was happening in the story, and what you were thinking about?"

I gave students a moment to think back and talk.

"Let's start by reading a chunk of the final part of this story. As I read, will you do the intellectual work that the story seems to be asking you to do? That is, will you think independently as we read, attending to the analytical work you've learned to do? To help with this, keep one eye on our anchor charts, use your notebook to jot, and stay alert to places you could try some of the work listed on them." I gestured to both charts as I spoke.

> **ANCHOR CHART**
>
> To Think Deeply about Characters . . .
>
> - Expect characters to be complicated and show more than one trait.
> - Revise your thinking in the face of new evidence.
> - Look at a character's less likeable sides.
> - Know that some traits matter more than others because they affect the rest of the story.
> - Consider the pressures exerted on characters.
> - Reflect on the characters and the story again, after you read the ending.

> **ANCHOR CHART**
>
> To Investigate the Influence of Setting on Characters . . .
>
> - Ask, "What kind of place is this?"
> - Consider the mood of the place.
>   - the atmosphere
>   - how people treat each other
> - Notice how the author's specific language evokes emotions and images.
> - Ask, "Is a character torn? Is something in the setting pulling a character between competing pressures?"
> - Investigate how the psychology of a place shifts, and how those shifts affect characters.

CONDUCTING THE READ-ALOUD

Read an excerpt from the second half of the story.

I read the excerpt shown aloud.

> During my walks from class to class I discovered that most of the eighth grade had taken sides and that my side consisted of me, a foreign exchange student named Hans, and two girls whose hearts I had not yet broken. The rest of my peers were massed behind Mike, eager to see me put in my place once and for all.
>
> The last class of the day was shop. We were all told by our teacher, Mr. Bledsoe, to work on our special projects. My special project was a skateboard, so I began sanding its nose and trying with all my might not to think about the fight. It is said that there is nothing like working with wood to take one's mind off a problem, but it could also be said that

> there is nothing like a problem to take one's mind off working with wood. No matter how intensely I sanded the nose of my skateboard, the fight was always with me, and the air around me seemed as thin as Alpine or Himalayan air.
>
> I tried to tell myself that in three hours it would all be over, that I would be in my own house, in my own room, and the fight would be a memory. But three hours would not be enough if I lost the fight. A month would not be enough to heal my humiliation. What would be enough? I asked myself. Six months? No. A year? Yes. A year would be enough. In a year I would be able to look back on this day and smile, or perhaps laugh. In a year the fight would be a distant memory, and I would be a different person with different friends and new reasons to feel confident and proud.
>
> So I closed my eyes and asked God to please make it a year later—to please take me out of this year and place me in the next. With my eyes closed I almost believed that time was racing past me, that eggs were being laid, chicks were being hatched, growing plump, laying their own eggs, and dying.
>
> Unfortunately, when I opened my eyes, I knew that I was still thirteen, still in shop class, and that the fight was waiting to be fought. I thanked God anyway, guessing I had prayed the wrong prayer, looked at the clock, and saw that I had ten minutes left. I did not even try to sand my skateboard those last ten minutes. Instead I drifted into a pleasant state of suspended animation where there was no joy, no fear, no pride, no regret. During this time my pulse rate and respiration dropped, the blood in my veins slowed to a crawl, and I believe I stopped aging.
>
> And then the bell rang, and my time was up.

"Share what you're thinking." Most kids spoke of Will's complicated character traits, as this part of the story highlights his complexity. Some talked of the pressure to be tough. Others said Will is becoming more anxious and how he handles fear by shutting down, rather than trying to change his situation.

After a moment, I said, "Readers, I hear you discussing Will—how complicated he is. We can definitely see that he is somehow trapped. He feels unable to put a stop to this fight even though he doesn't want it."

"What's important is that nobody had to tell you—think about character traits! Instead, you saw that the story gives you a lot of information about what's going on inside Will's head, and *those* details give you a lot of information about the kind of kid Will is. You're also getting good at embracing complexity. You don't try to simplify characters. You don't say, 'He's a jerk.' Instead, you say things like, 'He seems to feel pressured to be tough.' Your books have a lot of complicated characters, too."

Add in a new lens, that of considering how sometimes, characters also exert an influence on a place.

"Readers, when you talked about the pressure on Will, you were doing that work of thinking what kind of place this is, and how it affects characters. This school seems like the kind of place where a lot of kids act tough, not just Will. After all, it's not as if Mike says, 'Oh, no big deal,' and they can be friends.

"You know that places affect characters. Today, I want to alert you to the notion that the reverse is true, too. Characters affect places. They especially affect the mood, or psychology of a place, when they act as a group. I'm going to reread this last part. Listen with that lens of group psychology. See if you hear what I hear."

The invitation to guide their own thinking work increases students' agency—and the likelihood of transfer to their independent work.

If you are a humanities teacher, clearly historical references would be apt here. If your grade level is departmentalized, it might be helpful to let your social studies colleagues know you are studying the power of groups and individuals and find out if there may be parallels across the disciplines.

> During my walks from class to class I discovered that most of the eighth grade had taken sides and that my side consisted of me, a foreign exchange student named Hans, and two girls whose hearts I had not yet broken. The rest of my peers were massed behind Mike, eager to see me put in my place once and for all.

Demonstrate how you notice particular groups of characters, and think about how they may play a role in this place. Introduce the notion of the influence of group dynamics.

I read aloud again, slowly, "'. . . most of the eighth grade had taken sides . . . the rest of my peers were massed behind Mike . . .' Doesn't that sound ominous?"

I paused for emphasis, then said, "Readers, whenever characters begin to think and act alike, it can be a force for great good, or a force for evil, in books and in the world. Readers are alert, then, to the influence of group dynamics in a place, and the effect it may have on individual characters.

"As we read on, will you be extra alert for the influence of group dynamics? You may begin to see something else as well—the power of a group versus the power of an individual. Be alert to that tension, too. Have your notebooks out, so you can jot thoughts or phrases that seem significant." I showed my notebook where I had jotted "group dynamics" on one page and "versus the individual" on the opposite.

I read on, through ". . . fight whenever we were ready."

> We were to meet in front of the school. When I got there, I saw a crowd of fifty or sixty people awaiting my arrival. Under different circumstances I would have been pleased by the turnout, but the hopelessness of my position offset whatever theatrical lift I might have felt. I did, however, smile. I was, after all, the other half of the act and was not about to look somber or scared or penitent for anyone.
>
> I saw Mike Dichter standing fifteen or twenty feet away, looking as menacing as ever. He fixed his eyes on me for a moment, then kissed his girlfriend, Linda Lieban. I had foolishly broken up with Linda ten months before. Now, as Mike was kissing her, she looked at me as though she would soon have her revenge.
>
> And then, before I knew it, someone said, "Let's go," and everyone started walking toward the park two blocks away. Strangely, I felt not like a boy on his way to a fight but like a king on his way to the gallows. These were not my classmates before me but peasants in revolt. My wife had already been beheaded, my children sold for horses, my servants set free.
>
> I tried to put everything in perspective, to assure myself that it was only a fight and that losing was no disgrace. And maybe I wouldn't lose. Maybe I was one of those people who did not know his own strength until he was confronted.

> Maybe when I was facing Mike, some inherited ancient instinct would propel me toward his throat and give me the strength of ten men. My father was certainly a powerful man. My father, at certain times, was one of the most powerful and frightening men I knew. Up to that moment, all I thought I had inherited from him was his pride and his nose, but maybe once I was standing face-to-face with Mike Dichter I would discover that I had inherited his blind rage and lion heart as well.
>
> When we got to the park, a short discussion about the rules of the fight took place. First it was decided that kicking and biting should not be allowed, then that kicking should be allowed, but not scratching. During this time I was standing by a stone water fountain, breathing slowly and wondering when the blood of my father and his father and his father's father was going to show itself. I still couldn't summon enough rage or fury or indignation to make me want to fight Mike or anyone else. All I could do was hope that I was subconsciously feeling those things and was merely biding my time.
>
> "A fight's a fight," I heard someone say. "No bullshit rules."
>
> This motion was contemplated, then carried: Everything allowed. No bullshit rules.
>
> "Should we take our shirts off?" I asked, hoping to postpone things a little longer.
>
> "Whatever," someone said.
>
> And with that all the decisions were made, and there was nothing for Mike and me to do but face each other and fight. Tim Hamilton, our referee, walked us to a clearing and told us to shake hands and fight whenever we were ready. For a moment Mike and I just looked at each other. Then Mike crouched a little, I do not know why, and began to circle me. I knew I should move in and attack immediately, but I was rooted where I stood.

Swear word alert. You could substitute sissy. *Follow your norms.*

"Did you catch some nasty group dynamics? Think, look at your notes, or jot. Then think with your partner. What group dynamics did you see? Did you see conflict with the group versus the individual?"

I listened as students talked about "mob mentality"—how the eighth-grade kids were more vicious together than they probably were alone. Some noted the role Linda played, in egging on the fight. Others noticed how the rules were thrown out. Many kids began to talk about Will as a victim in this incident.

Sum up, and demonstrate how you make this thinking even more complicated, by considering the role of the individual, either for good as the leader, or for bad as a "bad apple."

"Fascinating! I heard you talking about the rather scary mob mentality this eighth-grade group demonstrates, how they seem to egg each other on, instigating this fight. Certainly the group seems to wield tremendous influence, and in this case, in this place, it's for bad, not for good.

"Now I'm going to add in thinking about the role of the *individual*. I heard you begin to think about Will as the victim of this group. In many stories, and in history, the individual can be the victim of a group. Sometimes, the individual might be a great leader and a force for good, like Dr. Martin Luther King Jr., in the world, or Katniss, in literature. But other times, an individual can be a force for bad. He or she can be what's called a 'bad apple' or sometimes 'a bad seed' if the character is truly evil. Will's not a bad seed, but he may be a bad apple. Research about bad apples shows that they can have a tremendously negative effect on a group, overwhelming otherwise positive norms!

"I'm thinking of a line from the beginning of this story." I made a show of finding it. "It says, 'Things probably would have taken a peaceful turn if I hadn't walked home with Kevin Cox after school and told him that the next time Mike and I played basketball I was really going to throw some elbows, and if he, Mike, didn't like it, I would fight him anytime, anywhere.' Hmm, . . . doesn't that sound like a bad apple? Maybe Will is . . . an instigator. Remember that later, Will talks about how he sat at lunch and . . . wait a minute, here's how he describes himself, 'talking and listening in my usual superior way.'

"So I think we need to hold both truths as coexistent—the group is influencing this place in a negative way through the power of group dynamics, and Will also has a negative influence as a bad apple."

Finish the story, channeling students to be alert for the power of group dynamics and the power of the individual.

"Readers, as we finish the story, can you prepare to discuss with your partner what force you think was most influential in this place, in this incident? Was it the power of group dynamics? Was it more the single bad apple? Or both? It doesn't look like we're going to see it, but if you suddenly see a powerful good leader, weigh that influence as well. It may not turn up here, but it will in some of your books."

"Ready? Do you need a second to set up any notes?" I jotted quickly in my notebook and held it up, with quick headings of "group dynamics," "bad apple," and "good leader."

I read on.

If you'd like to hear more about how a single "bad apple" in an otherwise positive group can overwhelm positive social or professional norms, listen to the first seven minutes of the podcast "Ruining It for the Rest of Us." In this episode of This American Life, *Ira Glass shares research on the ruinous effect "bad apple" behavior can have on morale, creativity, and productivity. It's enlightening.*

. . . Then Mike crouched a little, I do not know why, and began to circle me. I knew I should move in and attack immediately, but I was rooted where I stood.

"Fight!" someone said. And now Mike began to advance and kick karate style. The kicks not only served to display his formidable kicking skills but were also a superior defensive and offensive weapon. In order to get to Mike, I would have to find some way to get around his kicks, and in order to do that, I would have to be someone who knew how to fight. My only choice, therefore, was to look unworried and back up, which is what I did. Mike, however, was advancing steadily, which meant that I could either continue backing up until I reached the bus stop on Santa Monica Boulevard or stand my ground and see what happened. Pride demanded that I choose the latter, just in time for Mike to kick me on the thigh. I turned sideways to present a thinner target, bent my knees a little, and took a hard kick to the ribs.

SESSION 13: READ-ALOUD

And then things began to happen very quickly. In an instant Mike was on me, and my legs buckled, and we were wrestling on the ground. In an effort to prove that I could fight as dirty as anyone, I gingerly grabbed his groin and discovered that I had neither the will nor the strength to squeeze.

"So that's how you want to play?" Mike said, grabbing *my* groin a good deal less gingerly and wrestling me onto my back. Somehow I was able to get out from under him, and a great deal of grappling, kicking, scratching, and punching ensued while the crowd yelled for either Mike or me to do something that I could not quite make out. Then I saw blood on my shirt and wondered who was bleeding. Before I could find out, Mike was on top of me and my arms were pinned under his knees and he was hitting me very hard in the face. Curiously, I hardly felt the punches. All I felt was the dull impact of the blows, and all I heard were the shrieks and hollers of the crowd, along with the *thump, thump, thump* of fist hitting cheek, ear, chin, forehead, and occasionally mouth. For some reason I was very relaxed. Perhaps because I sensed that I was only getting what I deserved. After all, I had feasted on my own glory and egotism for three years. The check was bound to come.

"Kill him!" I heard Linda Lieban cry. "Kill him!" So Mike reached back and hit me on the side of the head with the hardest punch he had thrown yet.

"Give?" he said.

I shook my head.

"Okay," he said, reaching back to kill me again. He repeated this eight or nine times, and after each punch he said, "Give?" and I said, "No," or shook my head, and he reached back again.

And then, for an instant, I had had enough. For one brief moment the blood of my father and his father and his father's father welled up within me, and I put my hands under Mike's knees, lifted him in the air, held him there, and threw him off me. The crowd gasped, and for a moment Mike looked surprised, even scared. I stood up to my full height, and the full height of my pride and dignity, but I did not know what to do next. I was no more willing to fight now than I had been before; and the moment passed, and my fury ebbed, and before I knew it, Mike was on top of me picking up where he had left off.

Soon I could not distinguish one punch from another, and my ears burned, and the noises around me seemed to be coming from the other end of a hollow tube. I saw glimpses of faces, but I did not see friends or former friends—all I saw was a crowd, and all I heard was a crowd's noise. I knew it was all over—the love notes, the phone calls, the envy and adulation. Each punch robbed me of another friend, another heart, another follower. From here on out it would just be me, and my TV, and my memories of glory.

And then, one by one, or two by two, the lights went out in my mind, and Mike's legs were around my stomach and I couldn't breathe.

"Give?" he said.

I shook my head.

He squeezed harder. "Give?"

Why not? the last light in my mind said. *All I'm giving him is the fight.* So I gave: I gave him the fight, the love notes, the phone calls, the envy, the adulation, and the arrogant hull of who I had been.

For a moment I felt very light, almost weightless.

Remind students of their lenses and give them a moment to jot. Then invite them to compare influences in this place, this incident.

"Readers, take a moment to jot evidence for the influence of group dynamics. Evidence for bad apples. Evidence for good leaders." I gave them a moment. "Go ahead, compare!"

I listened in as students talked about Linda as another bad apple, of the hollers of the crowd, of Will calling himself an "arrogant hull."

It could also be interesting to study how this story ends and what the implications are of the final sentence—and why it's isolated as its own paragraph. I don't do it here because it would derail the work in hand, but it is interesting to ponder.

"Yikes! Scary! I agree with those of you who called Linda another bad apple! And that crowd mentality. They were more than bystanders, they were like a crowd of instigators. We definitely saw the power of group dynamics in how they pushed for this fight. At the end, we saw Will lose all his influence and power, didn't we?"

LINK

Channel students to read independently, trying this work in their own novels.

"We've come to realize that both group dynamics and powerful individuals can wield influence in a place. Sometimes, too, the group and the individual can be at odds with each other, which creates extra tension.

"Some of you will want to read this story again, and I have copies here. What will be even more interesting, though, will be to see how this plays out in your novels. In a longer novel, you may get several changes in who influences a place—power may shift from one group to another. I'm also curious how this may play out in your studies of history. You may not only see some bad apples, you may see strong leaders as well. As you go off to read today, add this to your repertoire." I added a new bullet to our anchor chart.

ANCHOR CHART

To Investigate the Influence of Setting on Characters . . .

- Ask, "What kind of place is this?"
- Consider the mood of the place.
  - the atmosphere
  - how people treat each other
- Notice how the author's specific language evokes emotions and images.
- Ask, "Is a character torn? Is something in the setting pulling a character between competing pressures?"
- Investigate how the psychology of a place shifts, and how those shifts affect characters.
- **Consider how group dynamics or powerful individuals may influence a place.**

Consider how group dynamics or powerful individuals may influence a place.

NO GIRLS ALLOWED!

SESSION 13: READ-ALOUD

INDEPENDENT READING

Check to see if students are doing high-level reading work in their own books.

As you move forward in the second bend, make sure that students are moving with you, applying this work to their own books. Sometimes during whole-class lessons kids seem to have internalized new work—but back at their desks, they revert to what they were doing before this new instruction. Many teachers note, for example, that the work students engage in during the read-aloud is remarkably high. But when they listen to students' club and partner talk, or look at their Post-its, the transfer is sometimes low, in that the high-level thinking from the read-aloud isn't visible in the students' independent work.

So today, you might move from student to student, pointing at your anchor charts and asking quietly, "Can you show me what reading work has been most significant for you?" You might tell students you'll return in a few minutes, so they can prepare to give a quick tour of their Post-its, annotations, or reading notebook. Or you could suggest that a partnership or informal club share their reading work, and you can listen in. Use this time for quick, informal assessment of students' response to instruction. If there's trouble, you won't have time to solve it now, but you can learn enough to plan which students you'll need to return to. You may also find students whose annotations, Post-its, or notebook entries you can use as mentor texts for others.

SHARE

Invite readers to share their reading work with each other.

"Readers, take a moment to talk to a couple of readers outside of your partnership to get ideas for your own work. Ask about the books they've been reading and their reading work. Talk about your own reading work. Use what you learn from other readers to help you to deepen or add to your existing reading plan, as tonight you'll set your own homework."

SESSION 13 HOMEWORK

READERS SET THEIR OWN HOMEWORK

Readers, today we read aloud the final part of "The Fight" and thought about ways that characters or groups of characters exert influence on the setting. Tonight, as you are reading your own books, will you set yourself some homework for the thinking work that you'll do, and will you make sure your jotting develops that thinking? You might choose among the strategies you've been learning to explore the relationship between the setting and characters, or return to strategies for tracing complicated character traits, depending on how your story is developing and the work you have set for yourself.

As always, aim to read at least thirty to forty pages, and jot for about five minutes. Be sure to record your reading on your reading log.

Session 14

Settings Also Change in Time, Often Bringing in Backstory to Develop the Character

IN THIS SESSION

TODAY YOU'LL teach students that settings may change in terms of time, often bringing in backstory to develop the character. Perceptive readers are alert to these time changes and how they give the reader added insight into the character.

TODAY YOUR STUDENTS will add this work to their repertoires, noticing moments when the author provides backstory to develop a character. They may use timelines as a method of taking notes to track shifts in time in their novels.

GETTING READY

✓ Prepare to show two video clips, "Potions Class at Hogwarts" and "Severus Snape: Important Scenes in Chronological Order." Links to these clips are available in the online resources (see Teaching and Active Engagement).

✓ Display and add to Bend II anchor chart, "To Investigate the Influence of Setting on Characters . . ." (see Link).

✓ You might want to show a timeline of story events to demonstrate time shifts (see Conferring and Small-Group Work).

✓ You might have on hand a story such as "Stray" by Cynthia Rylant with clear transitional phrases for time change (see Conferring and Small-Group Work).

✓ Be prepared to display, annotate, and discuss an excerpt from "One Holy Night" by Sandra Cisneros, from *Woman Hollering Creek* (see Share).

✓ You may also find the "Structure" strand of the Bands of Text Complexity in Literature from *A Guide to the Reading Workshop: Middle School Grades* helpful.

MINILESSON

CONNECTION

Get your readers interested in the notion of movement of time by calling to mind a character and story they know.

"Readers, I was watching a Harry Potter movie this weekend, and I was so struck by how certain scenes go back in time. I checked my Harry Potter books to see if this was in the original books, and yes, Rowling is constantly moving time around, giving you glimpses of earlier moments. It's like the author brings you back in time to teach you something. So, I thought that today we could investigate that together."

Name the teaching point.

"Today I want to teach you that one way that the setting may change in a narrative is that the time may change, often bringing in backstory to develop the character. Perceptive readers are alert to time changes and ask themselves, 'How does this backstory add to my understanding of this character?'"

TEACHING AND ACTIVE ENGAGEMENT

Engage students in an inquiry into the significance of backstory, using clips from Harry Potter to move back in time and investigate the character development of Professor Snape.

"Let's try this together. Let's do a mini-inquiry using Harry Potter, asking ourselves, 'What new information do we learn when the author brings us back in time, and what new insights does this give us into characters?'"

"When I was reading this weekend, I was struck by how mean Professor Snape could be to Harry. He seems like such a bully, and he's so hard on Harry, right from the start. Let's watch this scene, from the first book and movie, and you'll see what Professor Snape is like."

I played the first clip. Then I said, "Snape is so harsh with Harry! It's like he is against him before he even knows him."

Play the second clip, and invite partners to share their thinking.

"Now let's look at another clip. Harry is a little older, and he's upset because he is convinced that Snape hates him and his whole family—his mother, Lily, and his father, James Potter. So here, going back in time, we see Harry's mother and Snape when they were kids. Harry's mother is the girl with red hair. Snape is the boy with black hair. Let's see what we learn . . . And remember your question, 'What do we learn and what new insights do we have into these characters, from going back in time?'"

"What are you thinking? What did you learn about Snape and the Potters, from going back in time and seeing them when they were young?"

I listened as students noted how much Snape clearly liked Harry's mother, even loved her, and how her death devastated him. Others noted that Harry's dad was mean to Snape—and he looked a lot like Harry.

Summarize new insights and then remind students of the thinking work involved.

"Readers, it's interesting how we find out that Snape was really fond of Harry's mother. It's not that he didn't like her—he liked her a lot. Some of you noticed that Snape seemed more open and vulnerable when he was young. And we find out more perhaps, about why Snape doesn't like Harry's dad. That was James Potter with his friends, being so mean.

Shifts in time are one of the ways that novels become increasingly complex, and often young readers miss the small language cues that time has moved backward or forward. When there is white space and asterisks they (might) notice, but when the clues are changes in verb tense, they often miss these clues entirely.

"So Rowling put these scenes into the story for a *reason*. This movement in time doesn't just take us back to an earlier period for the heck of it. These time shifts give us some backstory. They give us new insights into Snape. These shifts in time develop Snape's character.

"If you notice time changing in your story, especially if it's a flashback, ask, 'Why did the author give me this glimpse into the past? What new insights do I have into the characters from this backstory?'"

LINK

Suggest that readers add this work to their repertoire, and suggest that it might deepen and extend their thinking work.

"Readers, it seems as if this will be interesting work for you to continue in your own books. If you're reading books where there are shifts in time, you might revisit those moments, reading more closely to consider why the author did that, and what new insights you gain about your characters. Sometimes authors give you backstory at the beginning of the book, and sometimes they give you bits of information across the story, in moments that take you back in time. Be alert to those moments and shifts in time."

I pointed to our anchor chart, where I'd recorded today's teaching, and said, "Readers, you have many choices about the reading work you might do today. Some of you can plan for work based on what you're most intrigued by, and some may need to see how your novel unfolds, to make decisions. Make sure you're reading alertly, paying attention to the small details that other, less alert or knowledgeable readers, might miss. Off you go."

ANCHOR CHART

To Investigate the Influence of Setting on Characters . . .

- Ask, "What kind of place is this?"
- Consider the mood of the place.
  - the atmosphere
  - how people treat each other
- Notice how the author's specific language evokes emotions and images.
- Ask, "Is a character torn? Is something in the setting pulling a character between competing pressures?"
- Investigate how the psychology of a place shifts, and how those shifts affect characters.
- Consider how group dynamics or powerful individuals may influence a place.
- **Pay attention to backstory to gain new insight into characters.**

Pay attention to backstory to gain new insights into characters.

CONFERRING AND SMALL-GROUP WORK

Tracing Time Changes in Novels
Alerting Readers to Cueing Systems for Time

WHEN YOU CONFER WITH READERS TODAY, you'll probably want to ask whether time has changed in their novels, and to help them notice ways that authors signal time changes to readers. Many young readers miss those cueing systems. That's especially important because changes in time are also one of the most common ways that texts become more complex—time becomes less linear, and the cues are less obvious. You might find the "Structure" strand of the Bands of Text Complexity in Literature helpful to ponder this.

Even obvious techniques such as date headings, white space, rows of stars, and transitional phrases may fly past your readers, even your more avid readers. You might consider two methods to help students see these cues. One way is to gather a small group of readers who are reading texts of the same level. Invite each student to find a few places where time changes. Then the small group could compare the different ways that the author lets the reader know time has changed. This inquiry could heighten students' awareness of these cues. When they return to their reading, they will probably be more alert to time shifts.

Some of your readers might find it helpful to do some guided practice, making quick timelines to capture how time moves in a story. You might demonstrate with a timeline from the beginning of *The Hunger Games*—just the big shifts in time.

Timeline from the Beginning of *The Hunger Games*

• Day of the Reaping
• Peeta is picked and Katniss thinks back to when she was starving and he gave her bread.
• Back to the Day of the Reaping
• On the train to the capital, Katniss flashes back, thinking about her father singing to mockingjays.

Show students how time moves back and forth even as the story moves forward, and that you can capture those moves using a timeline, which will also help you think and talk about why those time changes are included.

Another way to help your students notice cueing systems for time changes is to gather them around a shared reading text. Choose a short story in which there are clear transitional phrases that signal time shifts, such as in Cynthia Rylant's "Stray." Invite students to study the way the author signals jumps in time across the story. Then you could send students back to their own stories, asking them to notice how their author marked time changes.

SHARE

Noticing Rapid and Subtle Time Shifts through Verb Tense Changes

Ask students to notice verb tense changes and time shifts in a story, then discuss why the author included those time shifts.

"Readers, it used to be that the novels you were reading would alert you to time changes, with a lot of white space, or stars, or dates. They'll often still do that for big time changes. But authors also make a lot of rapid and subtle time shifts, sometimes even within a paragraph! One way they alert you to time changes is through the verb tense changing.

"Let's look, for example, at this passage from 'One Holy Night,' from Sandra Cisneros's *Woman Hollering Creek*. A girl is talking about a boy called Chaq. Will you study this passage with a partner? See how many times you see the verb tense changing . . . and then talk to your partner about how time changes in this passage."

> He said his name was Chaq. Chaq Uxmal Paloquín. That's what he told me. He was of an ancient line of Mayan kings. Here, he said, making a map with the heel of his boot, this is where I come from, the Yucatán, the ancient cities. This is what Bot Baby said.
>
> It's been eighteen weeks since Abuelita chased him away with the broom, and what I'm telling you I never told nobody, except Rachel and Lourdes, who know everything. He said he would love me like a revolution, like a religion. Abuelita burned the pushcart and sent me here, miles from home, in this town of dust, with one wrinkled witch woman who rubs my belly with jade, and sixteen nosy cousins.
>
> I don't know how many girls have gone bad from selling cucumbers. I know I'm not the first. My mother took the crooked walk too, I'm told, and I'm sure my Abuelita has her own story, but it's not my place to ask.

As students studied the text, I annotated it. After giving students a moment to talk, I gathered them back to explain. "It's so interesting! In the first paragraph, Cisneros takes readers back in time to the moment when the narrator met Chaq. 'He said his name was Chaq.' Past tense. Then in the next paragraph, she takes readers forward in time, to eighteen weeks after the narrator has been sent to live with her grandmother. 'What I am telling you . . .' Present tense. In the third paragraph, Cisneros moves back into past tense when she takes readers even farther

FIG. 14–1 It can be helpful to do shared close reading of a text like this and to timeline the shifts in time. Time changes are marked here by subtle shifts in verb tense.

SESSION 14: SETTINGS ALSO CHANGE IN TIME, OFTEN BRINGING IN BACKSTORY TO DEVELOP THE CHARACTER   **117**

back in time, giving a glimpse of the narrator's mother, and even a slight insight into her grandmother's life. The passage certainly contains layers of backstory!

"Readers, when you are reading books like *Holes*, *Delirium*, *My Sister's Keeper*, or *The Hobbit*, you'll have to be extra alert to the subtle ways authors change time."

SESSION 14 HOMEWORK

 ### NOTICING WHEN TIME CHANGES

Readers, tonight as you read, be extra alert to when time changes in your novel, and notice how your author lets you know that time has moved forward or backward. Does it move evenly—or are there jumps between chapters? Does time ever change within a chapter? Maybe even more often? Flag some of these pages. Dealing with time changes will help you be able to read harder novels, so practice some of this work tonight. As always, get as much reading done as possible, aiming for thirty to forty pages.

Tomorrow, we'll have a gallery walk of reading notebooks, and a partner reflection using reading logs. Make sure you are ready for that important work, as well.

Session 15

Readers Share Their Work and Reflect on Their Challenges and Growth

Dear Teachers,

Today marks the end of Bend II of the unit. A major and difficult goal of this bend was to coach students to tackle new reading work (attending to the interaction of setting and character) while continuing to do earlier reading work (analyzing complicated character traits) with increased automaticity. Your reader's notebooks should offer insight into how their thinking work is growing. Meanwhile, their logs should offer insight into how often they are in a reading zone, how they are doing with increasing volume, choosing books wisely, and keeping track of their reading.

Today, your day might not follow strict workshop timing, so that you can dedicate some time for students to attend to their notebooks, have a gallery walk, and have a reflective conversation. You might, then, teach a quick minilesson, teaching students that readers look for ways to reflect on how they are becoming more powerful thinkers, and that one window into their thinking will be the writing they do about reading. Sharing that writing about reading will be one way to share their thinking, and to inspire other readers with ways to deepen their thinking and notebook work.

Then you might give students some time to work on their reading notebooks in preparation to share a favorite page, as the knowledge that they are sharing their most powerful thinking sometimes leads readers to want to add to some of their work. You'll usually find students adding to earlier notebook work and/or creating some new work that shows their best thinking. While they're working, you can confer or offer small groups ways to use Post-its and notebooks to capture high-level thinking without having to write long, perhaps showing some mentor pages, or talking to students about the thinking they are most interested in and brainstorming ways to quickly develop and capture that. As they work, encourage them to draw on the anchor charts for Bends I and II, as well as the charts, "Optional Ideas for Your Reader's Notebook" (Session 12) and "Tips for Taking Your Writing about Reading from Good to Great" (Session 6).

Then have students lay their notebooks out, with some Post-its flagging pages that mark significant work. Invite students to do a gallery walk to study each other's notebooks. As they do, you can also walk around and quickly assess (perhaps jotting marks in your grade book), and/or you can walk around and audibly praise work that shows growth. Remember to not only reward neatness. Neatness and innovative thinking are not, in fact, correlated. So read some of that awkward handwriting and find some jewels in the notebooks of students who might find jotting hard, but whose thinking is significant. Sometimes it can be helpful to have students carry Post-its and nominate pages they think should go on a "notebook wall of fame" board, or get copied into a "class notebook of mentor pages" that readers can look to when they want ideas.

Next, you might have partners retrieve their notebooks and meet with another partnership, perhaps one with a similar course of study, to give tours of the thinking work they have done so far by pointing to pages and explaining them. The gallery walk helps students make their work public and gives them more ideas. The partner conversations and "tours" help them practice articulating reflective thinking using evidence and artifacts.

As a share today, you might invite students to get out their reading logs and give partners a tour of how reading has been going for them, by running their fingers across or down (depending on the tool they are using) their calendar or log, noting what books they were reading, how much they read, how often they were in the reading zone, and so on. Are they happy with their course of study? Are the books they've chosen leading them to read a lot? Do they need to solve any challenges? Invite them to reflect on their tool as well. Is it working? Does it make it easy to reflect? Do they want to stick with it or modify it?

At some point, ask partners to jot their specific goals for their future work. These could be goals about their reading notebooks, book choices, and/or fitting more reading in. To help, you might hand out mini-versions of the Bend I and II anchor charts, converted into checklists of sorts. Students can check off work they feel they do regularly, and can circle work they'd like to try more of as they move forward.

It's unusual to have a day in reading workshop when you have students write and talk more than they read. At this point, when students have done significant work, and if there is sufficient time, ask them to do some serious reflection. Of course, if there's time left after reflection, set them to reading!

All the best,
Mary

To Think Deeply about Characters . . .

- ☐ Expect characters to be complicated and show more than one trait.
- ☐ Revise your thinking in the face of new evidence.
- ☐ Look at a character's less likeable sides.
- ☐ Know that some traits matter more than others because they affect the rest of the story.
- ☐ Consider the pressures exerted on characters.
- ☐ Reflect on the characters and the story again, after you read the ending.

To Investigate the Influence of Setting on Characters . . .

- ☐ Ask, "What kind of place is this?"
- ☐ Consider the mood of the place.
  - ☐ the atmosphere
  - ☐ how people treat each other
- ☐ Notice how the author's specific language evokes emotions and images.
- ☐ Ask, "Is a character torn? Is something in the setting pulling a character between competing pressures?"
- ☐ Investigate how the psychology of a place shifts, and how those shifts affect characters.
- ☐ Consider how group dynamics or powerful individuals may influence a place.
- ☐ Pay attention to backstory to gain new insight into characters.

Analyzing Characters as Vehicles for Themes BEND III

A Letter to Teachers

Dear Teachers,

This is the final bend of our character study! By now, you're hopefully seeing two kinds of growth in your students. One is growth in their close reading skills—how they pay attention to detail and think analytically about their novels. Another is growth in how they manage their overall reading lives, making books central to their lives. The work of this bend continues to expand students' skills in both these areas.

So far, you've lingered in the work of studying character traits, character change, and the influence of setting on characters. Now, you'll move students into exploring how characters are vehicles for themes. You'll bring your readers first into the work of discerning motifs in their stories. Motifs can be thought of as subjects that an author is preoccupied with, ones that appear again and again in the story. They can also often be named in one word or a short phrase. For instance, "sacrifice" is a motif in *The Hunger Games*, as are "loyalty" and "betrayal." In our read-aloud text, "Popularity," "fitting in" is a motif, as is "loneliness."

What's lovely about motif work is that it is an easy bridge to theme. In this bend, you'll introduce students to the idea of tracing a motif across a text by asking readers to consider the troubles that characters face, noticing that some of those troubles surface more than once and become motifs in a story—they are subjects the author is interested in. Then, you'll move to considering what a story suggests about that motif and developing longer theme statements. You'll teach your students to ask, "What does this story suggest about loyalty?" Their theme statements may sound like, "Loyalty to friends can make you extraordinarily brave," or "Loyalty can lead to sacrifice."

Your students will have explored themes before in their chapter books. In the novels they are reading, there will be several themes, and some of them may even seem contradictory. For instance, in *The Hunger Games*, one theme is that "Loyalty can lead you to protect others," and another is "Loyalty can lead you to kill." The most important work is that your students begin to understand that great stories will be about more than one thing, and that great readers develop different kinds of thinking across a story.

Your middle school students should already recognize symbols, and even be able to trace them across a story. What gives middle school students significant trouble is linking symbols, or any author's craft, to thematic development. There are two big ways to go about this work so that it becomes manageable for middle school students. One way is to lead students to find places in their stories where a theme becomes visible, and then to consider what particular author's craft the writer uses there to develop a theme. This is sophisticated analytical reading work with deep connections to writing that will thread through books in the other reading units as well. Here, we also suggest a second, slightly easier way for students to link craft, such as symbolism, to theme. They'll trace places in their novels where they see symbols, especially symbols related to characters, such as the Mockingjay in *The Hunger Games*, or the oxygen tank in *The Fault in Our Stars*. Then, they'll consider if those places that develop symbolism also develop a theme.

You'll wrap up the unit with a repertoire read-aloud that asks for similar agency in students flexibly applying reading strategies. It's a rich, engaging experience, and you'll want to read over the session, and perhaps rehearse it first with some colleagues. There's a bit of an art to how you invite students to decide what's most fascinating at that point in the story, and then you name what they talk about as replicable reading work. You'll use large Post-its with some of the strategies you've taught as manipulatives (manipulatives are not just for math!). Be ready to listen hard to students and to have in mind what you hope to hear in terms of students doing three things: applying reading work you've taught, transferring reading work they've learned in prior years, and innovating the reading work that the text suggests (you'll jot their innovations on smaller Post-its). In addition to helping to develop students' metacognition about their reading work, it can become a kind of informal performance assessment of students' agency and independence, drawing from the reading work you've taught and their own ability to adapt and innovate.

From there, your readers will have an opportunity in the final session to reflect on their growth in different areas in "reflection and agency centers," where they'll use artifacts to do some thinking about their reading lives—how much they are reading, how they are becoming better study partners, how deeply and closely they read. They'll have opportunities to apply their new reading skills to a fresh digital narrative.

Your students should be beautifully set up to go on with genre studies, book clubs, and studies of social issues. They should know more about themselves as readers. They should be more thoughtful, engaged readers of narrative, who see more in the books they are reading and in the texts they encounter in the world around them.

All the best,
Mary

Session 16

Read-Aloud
Characters' Troubles Become Motifs in a Story

IN THIS SESSION

TODAY YOU'LL TEACH, through a read-aloud session in which you channel students to study a video alongside you, that perceptive readers explore motifs in stories, often by analyzing the troubles characters face, and considering how these conflicts become subjects or motifs in a story.

TODAY YOUR STUDENTS will delve into next steps in their character work: focusing on troubles or conflicts to grow ideas about possible motifs. They'll continue to use their notebooks as places to jot their thinking, develop ideas, and reflect. They'll begin to develop note-taking systems to track motifs toward the end of the session.

GETTING READY

- Prepare to show "You Belong with Me," the narrative music video by Taylor Swift, as a read-aloud/video-aloud. We suggest specific stopping points in the video, so you'll want to preview it, noting the places to stop in the read-aloud. (Stop 1, boy has just written "tired of drama." Stop 2, boy has just closed curtain. Stop 3, female protagonist left alone on bench. Stop 4, female protagonist on stands, shaking her head. Stop 5, ending). A link to the video is available in the online resources (see Connection, Conducting the Read-Aloud / Video Aloud).

- Display Bend I and II anchor charts, "To Think Deeply about Characters . . ." and "To Investigate the Influence of Setting on Characters . . ." (see Connection).

- Students should bring their notebooks and Post-its to the meeting area (see Conducting the Read-Aloud / Video-Aloud, Independent Reading, and Share).

- Prepare sticky notes with literary words to describe characters: *Troubled, Frustrated, Competitive, Concerned* (see Conducting the Read-Aloud / Video Aloud).

- You might want to have word charts available of literary vocabulary for character traits (see Conducting the Read-Aloud / Video-Aloud).

- Write title on chart paper, "Possible Motifs in 'You Belong with Me.'" Have sticky notes on hand to jot students' ideas on possible motifs to add to this chart (see Conducting the Read-Aloud) / VIdeo Aloud.

- Introduce and display Bend III anchor chart, "To Investigate Themes" (see Link).

CONNECTION

Review the reading work students have done so far, and introduce the study of characters as vehicles for thematic development.

"I've been thinking about the reading work that you've been doing. You've been working hard to fit more reading into your lives, and to make smart book choices, to choose a course of books that go together, and that will move you forward as readers. You've also been thinking about the stories you've been reading, especially the characters, and the settings they inhabit, in nuanced and sophisticated ways.

"Over the next few days, let's extend our character study to think about how characters become vehicles for themes. Authors often use characters, including their traits and their troubles, their complicated relationships with each other and with places in the story, to develop themes across the story. In other words, studying characters can lead to deeper understanding of themes, and vice versa, studying themes can lead to deeper understanding of characters."

Introduce the video text. Channel kids to watch and listen, attentive first to details that suggest character traits, and then to details that suggest characters' troubles that might become motifs in the story.

"Today we will read a digital text together—it's a narrative music video. And yes, I used the word *read* on purpose, because when we study a digital text like a video, we think about it, we *read* it, just as we would read a print text. Some of you know it well, some may know the song but not the video, and some may have never heard or seen it. Let's read it today not as a music video, but as a narrative. You should see a lot of things that others would miss, because you have become such sharp readers.

"I know you'll continue to do the analytical thinking work you've been honing." I pointed to our anchor charts. "I'm guessing that thinking about character traits and setting will be important at the beginning of the story. Let's see what you notice. Then, let's be alert for the first moment when we begin to see troubles or conflicts, as those might become motifs in the story.

"The story begins with two characters, a male protagonist and a female protagonist. They live in houses across from each other, and the story begins with each character upstairs in his or her room. Let's see what you notice about these characters, right from the start."

CONDUCTING THE READ-ALOUD / VIDEO-ALOUD

Invite students to practice familiar thinking work about characters. Encourage them to support their ideas with evidence and to use literary language.

I played the beginning of the story, stopping at twenty seconds, right at the point where the boy character has written, "tired of drama" on his pad. Then I said, "I'm sure you have some thoughts on these characters. Talk to your partner. What are you thinking so far? Practice the work you know how to do."

I listened to students talk about how the boy seemed troubled or frustrated, and the girl seemed attentive, concerned, nice. I reminded them of the work we had done at the start of the unit, and coached them to weigh ideas and to use their literary vocabularies to come up with exactly the right words to describe the characters' traits. I jotted the words on different-colored Post-its and stuck them near the screen.

[Troubled]   [Competitive]   [Frustrated]   [Concerned]

Give specific feedback on use of literary language, reserving judgment, and supporting ideas with evidence.

"Readers, I want to give feedback on your work so far. What's strong about your work is that you're inferring traits and emotions from small details. I also hear you using two kinds of language. One is literary language. You didn't just say, 'He's unhappy.' You said, 'He's troubled.' You didn't just say 'nice.' You said 'compassionate.'" I gestured toward our literary word banks for character traits.

"You also used 'mitigated,' or 'measured,' language like 'so far . . .' and 'it seems like.' That reflects careful, reserved judgment, as it would be hard to know yet whether some of these are traits or emotions. You're wondering, is this boy usually frustrated? Or is he frustrated right now, for reasons we don't know yet?"

I paused, then challenged students. "There is still another way that you could raise the level of your thinking enormously. You know what I'm going to say. Don't nod at your partner. Don't just agree. Ask, 'What makes you say that?' Expect to share your idea . . . and your evidence."

Invite students to watch the clip again, this time more closely, gathering specific evidence for their ideas.

I started the video. "This time, watch more closely, looking for how you'd describe these characters—and also for the strongest evidence. You might choose one character and one word, for instance, and watch closely looking for evidence of that. I might look for evidence that this girl is 'concerned.' It'll be important, before we explore motifs, for you to be skilled at supporting ideas with evidence.

"Take a second, and make a plan with your partner for reading more closely. Do you want to divide up, and one of you will find evidence for the male protagonist's traits or emotions, and one will do the female? Or do you want to find evidence for different aspects of one character?"

I waited a moment for students to make a plan, then played the video again, to the point just after the boy closes the curtain and she is left staring at him (thirty-three seconds).

"Go ahead, share with your partner. What evidence did you gather to support your ideas? What details stood out as important this time?"

Analyzing Traits		
jovial cheery satisfied content	supercilious arrogant condescending proud	self-effacing unassuming modest shy
miserable despondent dejected forlorn	benevolent compassionate thoughtful caring	heartless malicious brutal spiteful
assertive self-assured poised confident	shrewd discerning perceptive insightful	chivalrous gallant considerate polite

FIG. 16–1 Word charts for character traits and for mood help students become more nuanced in their language.

I listened in and then summed up. "Readers, you're being much more specific. I heard one partnership, for example, suggesting that the boy seemed troubled, and their evidence included: 1) the way he walks around the room with the phone held tensely to his ear, his posture all tight and angry; 2) his facial expression, with his brow all furrowed; and 3) what he writes, 'tired of drama.'"

Define *motif*, then introduce the notion that a possible first step to thinking about themes is to study characters' troubles that repeat, and to consider whether these are motifs in a story.

"Let's keep going. We've done the reading work readers always do at the start of a story. We have a sense of who these characters are now. Let's shift to the new reading work of analyzing these characters and this text to search for possible themes. A great entry point to thinking about theme is to identify possible motifs. A motif is a subject that a writer returns to often, that appears again and again in the story. They're often named in one word or a short phrase. In *The Hunger Games*, motifs might be 'sacrifice' or 'loyalty' or 'betrayal.' In the story 'Popularity,' motifs might be 'fitting in' or 'ruthlessness.'"

Set up students to look for repeated troubles, then to consider motifs. Play the next part of the video.

"Let's give this a try. As you watch the next section, look for troubles or conflicts that are hiding in the story. Look for troubles that might be secret and harder to see—not just big, obvious ones."

"Then, try the work of moving from troubles to possible motifs. To identify possible motifs, readers often analyze the troubles that characters face, and then look for troubles that repeat. If a character faces the same trouble or conflict over and over, if the author seems preoccupied with that kind of trouble, then it may be a motif in the story."

I played the video right until the girl in the red convertible drives away, leaving the female protagonist alone on the bench.

Collect students' ideas, and use these as lenses to investigate possible motifs.

"I can tell you're dying to talk to each other. I'm so curious about what kinds of troubles or conflicts you noticed. Go ahead, talk with your partner."

After a minute, I paused the students. "Readers, it's significant that you saw troubles that are kind of secret and hard to see. It's easy to see this girl has a crush, but it's not so easy to see that shyness might be getting in her way, or that maybe this is the kind of place where fitting in or being popular really matters, and she's trying to find herself."

Donna Santman, author of Shades of Meaning: Teaching Comprehension and Interpretation in Middle School, *suggests that it can be helpful to coauthor interpretations with students as a way to elevate their thinking. Often, once you've helped them get started with more sophisticated thinking, they can go on with it.*

"Let's take this work to the next step, considering which of these may be motifs in the story. Turn and talk to each other. What troubles seem to come up across the story? What issues does the author seem preoccupied with?"

"I'll try to collect what you're saying on this chart." I unfolded a mini-chart labeled "Possible Motifs in 'You Belong with Me.'" As students talked, I added Post-its to the chart.

Demonstrate how you gather evidence for a motif, which may have both positive and negative aspects.

"To investigate motifs, I usually choose two or three possibilities to investigate across a story. If you only choose one, you could be stuck, because sometimes a conflict or trouble that seems powerful at the beginning doesn't continue to appear across the story. If you choose four or five, it's hard to trace them.

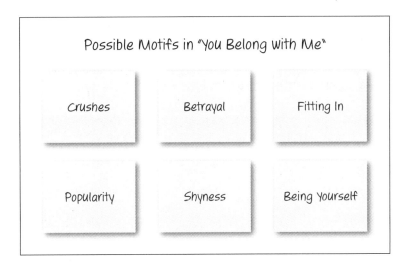

FIG. 16–2 A classroom chart on possible motifs

"So, how about . . . 'betrayal,' and 'being yourself'? Those are two big conflicts that seem likely to appear again since this boy seems to have little sense of loyalty, and the girl seems a bit conflicted about whether or not being herself is working out for her.

"Watch me do this work with the motif of betrayal. I'm looking for places in the story where this subject comes up. The first place I see betrayal . . . possibly . . . is when the boy closes the curtain on the girl. He was happy to write her notes and to get her sympathy, but he doesn't want to give her more. I see that as possibly a small betrayal.

"The next place I see possible betrayal is when the boy sits on the bench with our heroine, and plays with her hair. We know he has a girlfriend, because she pulls up in this fancy red car. That seems like major betrayal, of love, of loyalty, of relationships. So now I have two pieces of evidence, and the second is a lot stronger.

"Finally, I possibly see betrayal in the look between the two girls. At first, I thought the snotty way the dark-haired beauty looks at our heroine is a betrayal of girl loyalty. Why is she mean to the girl? It's her boyfriend who is straying! But then I thought of our heroine. She knows everything about this boy. She must know he has a girlfriend, yet there she is, writing him notes and sitting on benches with him. This third piece of evidence seems . . . complicated. I want to give it further thought."

In their great introduction to close reading, Falling in Love with Close Reading, *Kate Roberts and Chris Lehman show how choosing any lens, and reconsidering the text through that one lens, leads you to pay more attention to detail. Here, you apply that method and push students to read with more than one lens at a time.*

There are, of course, a thousand things to say about this text through the lens of critical literacy. Like so many Disney texts, this one suggests that girls are most successful when they are also long-haired and slender, and that what they want more than anything else is a boy—whom they somehow know is right for them from the most superficial evidence. If you go on to teach the unit on social issues book clubs, you may want to return to this text with the lens of oppressive gender norms and heteronormativity.

SESSION 16: READ-ALOUD

Debrief, then give students a chance to try motif work by exploring a second motif in partnerships. Give feedback to help readers lift the level of their work.

"See how I moved across the story, collecting moments when this motif appears? Some of my evidence was weaker, some was stronger, and some was complicated.

"Try exploring the motif of 'being yourself' with your partner. Name all the places that offer evidence of the motif. Then, you might weigh your evidence a bit, like I did. What's your strongest evidence? What evidence is complicated?"

After a couple of moments, I interrupted. "I'm listening to you and want to coach you a bit. Looking at conflicts or troubles is a way to help you get started. When you investigate a motif, you are looking for a subject that keeps coming up, for good or for bad. It's not necessarily linked only to one character, nor does it stay as a trouble for only one character. Keep going."

I gave students some more time to talk, then summed up their conversations. "Better. I heard you talk about how 'being yourself' comes up as a motif in scenes with both the female and male protagonists. Some evidence for this motif included the way the girl seems to explore different parts of herself, with all the outfits she tries on. Other evidence seems to be the way the boy is so different with the one girl than with the other, as if *he* hasn't figured out how to be himself. Interesting. So both these motifs are coming up across the story.

"What's important here is that you aren't thinking a motif is only linked to one character, or is only bad or only good. You're thinking of it as a subject that comes up again and again, in interesting ways."

Read on, continuing to collect evidence for motifs, giving some tips on setting up notebooks for jotting first.

"Let's go on. So far we've traced the possible motifs 'betrayal' and 'being yourself.' Plan to trace two motifs with your partner across the rest of the video. Do you want to stick with these two, or was there another one that interested you? Remember, if you choose a different motif, you need to think back over the beginning of the story to gather your evidence. Talk to each other and make a quick plan."

I gave students a moment to commit. Then I said, "It's worth it to take a second to set up your notebook for quick jotting, so you can hold onto your thinking. You might sketch a timeline and put your first motif on top and the second below, then mark places and jot notes on the timeline to represent where each

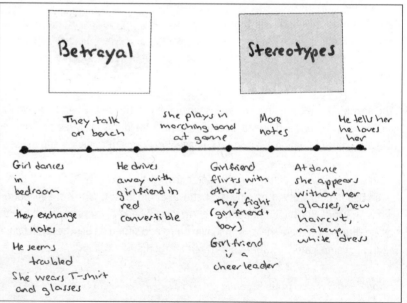

FIG. 16–3 Tracing motifs across the text. Using Post-its with a timeline allows the reader to change the motif, to test out a new lens across the story.

motif appears. Or you might make a simple T-chart, using Post-its to jot evidence that goes under each section of the T-chart, and move those around as you rank them. Set yourself up to hold onto your evidence."

I played the video to where the football game ends. The female protagonist is in the stands, shaking her head, and then the boy is back in his bedroom, preparing to leave for the dance (two minutes, forty-seven seconds).

Give partners a moment to think and jot, then share their thinking. Give feedback that motifs don't appear in *every* scene.

"Take a moment to jot notes to hold onto your thinking." I waited a few moments. "Go ahead, compare with your partner. Which motifs are playing out most strongly? What is your strongest evidence?"

I listened as partners found more evidence for "betrayal." Partners looking for more evidence for "being yourself" were a little stuck with finding new evidence. I reminded partners who had chosen new motifs to think back to the beginning of the text, as well.

"Readers, I'm listening in. What's going well is that you're gathering evidence, and you're holding onto it with fast note-taking. I can also tell that there is a little trouble with how often your motif appears. Sometimes, you're finding evidence for your motif in almost every scene. Other times, you'll have whole scenes, like chapters in a novel, when your motif doesn't appear, but it could still be important. A motif doesn't have to appear in *every* scene. It just needs to be an important subject across the story."

Play the video to the end, then invite students to weigh evidence and evaluate how motifs play out across the story.

"So let's go on with the story, and see if in the final scene, your motif appears again."

I played the rest of the video. There were murmurs, some of pleasure and some of frustration, when the female protagonist appears at the dance without her glasses, carefully made up and coiffed, in a white dress, and is finally "seen" by the male protagonist.

"I know there's a lot to say about how this story ends! There are ways it seems lovely, and ways it is also highly problematic. Right now, think of your motifs. Jot more evidence. Did your motif play out at the end? In any complicated ways?"

I gave students a few minutes to jot and think. Then, I channeled them to share with each other. After a moment, I said, "Readers, now, take a moment to sort and rank your evidence. What's the strongest evidence? What's complicated? What are you beginning to realize?"

After a couple of minutes, I called the students back together to summarize.

While I know it will be good to return to this text later with more critical literacy lenses, and I also hate to destroy children's idols, it feels impossible to let it pass that this text reiterates oppressive gender norms. So, while I don't spring that theoretical language on students (yet), I do want to suggest that there is a lot more to say about this text. If you've already got a discourse of critical literacy up and going in your classroom, then have at it now. Otherwise, know that in the next session we revisit the lessons in this text more critically.

"Readers, I hear you talking about how your motifs played out across the story. One partnership discussed how there was betrayal again in the scene on the playing field, when the dark-haired girl—let's call her our antagonist—flirts with another football player. Another partnership listed that as evidence of betrayal, but thought it was about equal in strength to the way the boy plays with the heroine's emotions. Hmm!

"Here's something super-interesting. This partnership traced the motif of being yourself. When the heroine appears at the end, having removed her glasses, done her hair, and changed her look, you know what they thought? That in changing herself she betrayed herself! So they found another example of betrayal, even as they were looking for evidence of being yourself. This is why it's interesting to talk to other readers. Together, you see more than you do alone."

LINK

Channel students to begin to do this reading and thinking work with motifs in their own novels.

"Readers, the most important thing about the work that you just did is this—you didn't wait until the end of the story to ask, 'What is this story beginning to be about?'

"If you wait until the end of a story, your thinking will often end up being just about what happens at the end. Instead, you looked for troubles that were hiding in the story right from the start, and you investigated these as possible motifs across the arc of the story.

"Then you reread and read on, gathering evidence for these motifs, realizing that a motif isn't related to only one character, and isn't necessarily always good or bad, and it isn't necessarily in every scene or every part of a story. Next, you weighed and evaluated your strongest motifs and strongest evidence—and you even found that some motifs were interrelated!

"Lots to think about! This work will be fascinating in other stories, too. See if any of the same motifs appear in your own novels, and what other motifs are particular to your novel. Add this work to the possible thinking work you might do."

ANCHOR CHART

To Investigate Themes . . .
- **Consider how characters' conflicts become motifs.**

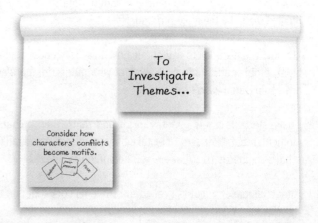

INDEPENDENT READING

Supporting Students in Beginning to Read for Motifs

Today, as always on read-aloud days, your students won't have long to read. Some students will be starting new books, some will be midway, and some will be finishing. It's important that students remember to do all the reading work they've learned, not just today's lesson—and to understand that some character trait and setting work is more important to do at the start of the story than, say, theorizing about possible motifs. You might circulate quickly, reminding students who are just beginning a book of the work they did with character traits and the way that settings affect characters. Invite them to think how they can continue that work and also raise the level of it, perhaps by extending the work to minor characters, or reading across a few chapters and thinking which particular focus would lead to the most interesting thinking work in their book.

For students who are midway through their books, or near the end, they can dive into motif work. You might suggest they spend a few minutes considering possible motifs, and then skimming back through their book to find which ones end up being particularly intriguing. You might also suggest that partners take a few minutes to think how they'll use Post-its and their reading notebooks to help keep track and gather evidence for possible motifs.

SHARE

Channel students to consider how to use Post-its and the reading notebook in interesting ways when tracing ideas about motifs, or any ideas, across a story.

"As you were reading today, some of you were beginning to jot possible motifs in your notebook, and some of you were jotting a few motifs on one Post-it. It would be worth it to take a moment to think, 'When I'm tracing a few ideas across a story, how do I want to use Post-its and my notebook?' Perhaps you want to use small Post-its of different colors for two or three motifs, and mark the places in your book where you see these most strongly. Then you might move those Post-its into your notebook, on a timeline, and think about which emerge more strongly in certain parts of the story. Or maybe you want to flag some pages as you read. After several chapters, look back, think, and write longer in your notebook about why one motif becomes extra important. This point is—consider how you'll use your tools to deepen your thinking over many pages, not just about motifs, but about any idea you trace across a story."

SESSION 16 HOMEWORK

COLLECTING EVIDENCE TO SUPPORT MOTIFS

Readers, today we began a new bend in our unit. Tonight for homework, continue the work we began today—noticing and tracking possible motifs. You might be starting to read a book from the course of study you planned earlier. You might ask, "What is this story beginning to be about?" You might also make note of characters' troubles that recur through the text. In addition, start a system for tracking possible motifs and for gathering evidence to support them. This might be as simple as flagging pages that suggest a particular motif. Or, you might jot quick bullet lists in your notebook naming possible motifs and listing evidence. Just be sure that your writing doesn't take up too much of your reading time. Aim to read for at least forty minutes, jot for about five, and record your reading.

Session 17

Moving from Motifs to Themes

IN THIS SESSION

TODAY YOU'LL teach students that by studying what an author has to say about a motif, readers can start to develop ideas about themes.

TODAY YOUR STUDENTS will practice moving step by step from motifs to themes, through exploring motifs further and reexamining relevant scenes in their books. They'll consider ways to use tools such as timelines and Post-its to track possible themes and develop their ideas.

GETTING READY

- Students should have their notebooks to discuss their homework with partners (see Connection).
- Be ready to show some moments from the Taylor Swift video, "You Belong with Me." A link to this video is available in the online resources (see Teaching).
- Display chart, "When Moving from Motifs to Themes, Ask . . ." (see Teaching).
- Display yesterday's motif chart, "Possible Motifs in 'You Belong with Me'" (see Teaching).
- Display chart, "How to Move from a Motif to a Theme, Step by Step" (see Teaching and Active Engagement).
- Display and add to Bend III anchor chart, "To Investigate Themes . . ." (see Link).
- Be ready to show some students how to trace motifs and themes using Post-its and a timeline. You may also want to provide or co-create a "trouble wall" of words to help develop motifs or themes (see Conferring and Small-Group Work).

MINILESSON

CONNECTION

Remind students of the work they did with motifs for homework last night, and give them a chance to share with a partner.

"Readers, last night you did some thinking and jotting about motifs in your books so far. Take a moment to share with your partner what you've come up with, including systems you're developing for tracing motifs and tracking evidence. Have your notebook open as you talk, and point to some of the work you did."

I gave students a few minutes to talk, and I circulated rapidly, making note of their work.

"Readers, one interesting thing I'm hearing as you talk is that similar motifs are coming up in books that seem really different. One partnership put together a course of study of coming-of-age/dystopian stories. They read the Gone series and they're currently reading The Maze Runner series. One motif they're interested in is 'survival,' a huge subject of that novel. That motif also came up in a completely different course of study, where the readers are reading *The Fault in Our Stars*, *A Child Called It*, and *My Sister's Keeper*, which are all about dealing with physical anguish.

"Readers, the motif of survival comes up in these books, but what the author has to say about that motif might be very different. I'm thinking, for instance, that *The Maze Runner* may have some different things to teach about survival than, say, *My Sister's Keeper*."

♣ **Name the teaching point.**

"Readers, today I want to teach you one way that readers might move from motifs to identifying possible themes in stories. They ask themselves: 'What does the author suggest about this motif?' Then, they develop a theme statement."

TEACHING

Offer ways to question the text about motifs, which can help students develop theme statements.

"There are a few tips to doing this kind of thinking work. I bet you already know some of them. Listen as I list a few ways I move from thinking about motifs, or one-word subjects, to coming up with theme statements. Listen and think, which of these have you done before? Are there any that seem a little new?

"These are some ways I move from motif to theme." I unfolded a chart as I spoke.

"Readers, to get to a theme statement, you're trying to figure out what the author has to say about this motif, and you want to say it as a sentence. It doesn't have to be long, but it's more than one word. For example, if I'm wondering what the author has to say about 'survival' in *The Maze Runner*, I can ask, 'What big lessons does the main character learn about survival?'"

I motioned that partners could talk to each other. "Have you done some of this work before? When? What's an example of it? Is some of it new or intriguing to you?"

I gave students a moment to talk, then gathered them back.

"Readers, a lot of you are saying that you've done work in the past with the first and third points on our chart—lessons characters learn and overarching messages or morals. You'll find this kind of thinking work interesting in the books you're reading now, too. This will help you move from naming a motif—to thinking about what the author has to say about that motif."

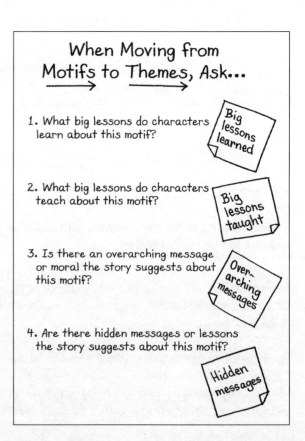

When Moving from Motifs to Themes, Ask...

1. What big lessons do characters learn about this motif? *Big lessons learned*

2. What big lessons do characters teach about this motif? *Big lessons taught*

3. Is there an overarching message or moral the story suggests about this motif? *Overarching messages*

4. Are there hidden messages or lessons the story suggests about this motif? *Hidden messages*

Invite readers to think alongside you as you choose a familiar motif from a familiar story, and then you choose a question that might help you explore a theme statement.

"Readers, let's try this using our story from yesterday's video read-aloud. Let's explore what the author has to say about one motif we explored: 'being yourself.'" I returned to our motif chart from yesterday and pulled one Post-it from it, "Being Yourself."

"Think with me as I try the fourth question on our motifs to themes chart, 'Are there hidden messages or lessons the story suggests about this motif?'

"To answer the question, I'll think back to the moments in the story when we saw that motif. As I retell those moments to myself, I try to explain what hidden messages or lessons might be in that scene. Think back along with me."

Play the video from the previous session, this time without sound, and demonstrate how you think back across the story, searching for hidden messages or lessons.

I played the video, without sound, to show visual clips.

"Here's what I'm thinking. First, I'll study the moment when the heroine was dancing in her bedroom, trying on different outfits and crazy hairdos. Hmm, . . . let me try to explain that, what might be a hidden message here . . . so maybe the author is saying . . . well, she's trying on all these different outfits, so maybe the author is saying it's hard to figure out who you even are, that high school is a time when kids struggle with identity? Does that make sense to you?"

I waited for nods. "And then . . . when she's standing on the sidelines in her band costume, and she realizes the boy doesn't even see her. Hmm, . . . let me explain how this might have some important hidden message . . . maybe . . . because when she's herself, it's like she's invisible?" I fast-forwarded, musing as I did so, and then stopped at the moment when the girl changes herself totally to go to the dance. "And then . . . there's the final scene, where she takes off her glasses and fixes her hair . . ."

I turned to students and said, "I can see you have some thoughts about that. Partners, one of you try to explain to the other . . . why might that scene, where she takes off her glasses and fixes her hair and makeup and comes to the dance, be important to our question, 'Are there any hidden messages here about this motif, being yourself?'"

I gave students a moment to talk and then gathered them back.

Share how you think about what the author might be saying overall about this motif or subject. Say your statement as a sentence, then support it with text evidence, using scenes from the story.

"Readers, listen as we try to put this together into a theme statement. We have one scene where it feels like the author shows that it's hard to be yourself. Our evidence is that the girl tries on all these different 'looks' likes she's trying to find herself. Then we have a scene where it feels like the author says sometimes it's hard to be yourself and be visible, and our evidence is that scene where she is in the stands in her band costume. And then there's the final scene, where you, like me, were saying that the author seems to suggest that it's hard not to change yourself for love."

I looked up and said, "So . . . it feels like a theme in this story that is sort of a hidden message is that *it's hard to be yourself*." I jotted that on a larger Post-it. "In this story, the author seems to suggest that it's hard to be yourself because of all the outside pressures to be a different way, because you can feel invisible and you feel like you have to change.

"You know what I just realized, readers? It's like you make a little essay when you try to explain how each part of the story matters."

Recap the work you just did as a series of replicable steps, then share a chart to solidify today's teaching.

"Did you see how to do this work, we first chose a motif we found interesting?" I asked, pointing to a chart that summarized the steps in our work. "Then we thought about a question we could ask about that motif. Next, we went back to the moments in the story when we saw that motif, with that question in mind, and we tried to explain why those parts might be important, thinking hard about what the author might be saying about that motif. Finally, we tried to say that idea as a theme statement."

ACTIVE ENGAGEMENT

Give readers a chance to do some preliminary thinking about theme statements in their novels.

"Readers, it's your turn to try this out in your own books. Will you open your notebook and remind yourself of the motifs you traced last night?" I gave them a moment to recall.

Pointing to our chart, "How to Move from a Motif to a Theme, Step by Step," I asked, "If you were to do this same work, thinking about lessons, messages, and morals, what question would you pose that would help you get to a theme statement?" I paused briefly, then asked, "Or do you already have some ideas about a theme statement? And are there parts of the story that seems important? Think for a moment, then share with your partner."

I listened as readers talked about lessons that Thomas learned about survival in *The Maze Runner*, and hidden messages about survival in *My Sister's Keeper*. I heard kids trying out preliminary ideas for theme statements, such as, "Struggling to survive can make you ruthless," and "When you feel alone, you don't always want to survive." I also noticed if students looked just at their notes, or if they opened their books.

LINK

Channel students to move from studying motifs in their books to exploring themes, reminding them that good stories will have more than one theme.

"Readers, let's send you off to work. One crucial point. Remember that you're not looking for the 'right' theme. Good stories will be about more than one theme. You're looking for themes that you find intriguing or significant. When you go off to work today, if you're not just starting a book but are a bit into it, you're probably ready to move from studying motifs to exploring larger themes. If you do, you might find some of these questions helpful." I pointed to the questions on our chart, "How to Move from a Motif to a Theme." "Or you might already have an idea for a theme statement, and you might test it out by gathering specific text evidence, which will mean some rereading and jotting.

"Readers, whether you are exploring themes, motifs, settings, or character traits, remember two things. First, just as there will be several traits for your character, and several ways the setting matters, there will also be more than one theme that a story suggests. And second, remember the work you've been doing in noticing the particular language the author uses, and using your notebook to collect some of that language. You'll find that your thinking is much more specific to the book you are reading, when you look again at the author's words.

"Take a moment to plan your work today. Are you early in your novel, collecting character traits and ideas about setting? Or are you farther along, so you can start to look for motifs, asking yourself what this story is beginning to be about and then asking yourself what the author suggests about these motifs?"

I pointed to our anchor chart and suggested partners make a plan before going off to read.

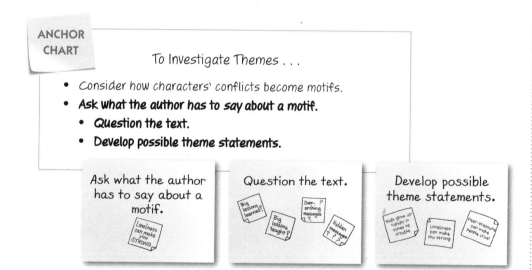

CONFERRING AND SMALL-GROUP WORK

Using Timelines and Post-its to Trace Motifs and Themes

TODAY YOU MAY WANT TO GUIDE STUDENTS to use tools to trace motifs and themes across their novels. You might pull a partnership that is fairly early in the book—the first third—and investigate the motifs they have found so far. Jot these motifs on small Post-its as they name them. Show how they might begin a timeline of major moments in the novel, using their notebooks or a large piece of paper. They can place each motif Post-it above the first place it appears on the timeline. They can keep tracking motifs by jotting on Post-its and placing them on the timeline, seeing how often each appears. This tool helps kids trace motifs across their novels. If students have grown initial thoughts on themes, they might also track themes across their novels on a timeline. Often, an idea for a motif or theme they committed to at the beginning of the story doesn't play out across the novel, or they'll find that some ideas only appear in one scene.

You might invite students who find this tool helpful to teach it to another partnership. Your emphasis is not only on teaching students to trace motifs and themes, it's on teaching students to peer confer. To do this, teach students that they have a few important steps. They need to explain the work and to give a quick example, often using a quick tool. Then they need to watch other students try it out and offer feedback. You might come up with predictable feedback about places where students often struggle, such as committing to a motif or theme that only appears in one scene, or committing to only one motif or theme, and not knowing if that one will play out across the novel. Set your first students up to rehearse how their peer conferring will go, and then send them off to work with another partnership.

Chances are good that many of your students will think the work of finding a theme in a book is work that readers do later in the text. You'll probably want to convey that actually, readers begin thinking about the theme of a book early on. They just do this in hypothetical ways, thinking, "Perhaps this is about . . ." or thinking, "Then again, it might turn out to be teaching readers that . . ." You have several options for how you can get that message out to your readers who are early in their books. One way is to gather those readers together in a small group—it could be a fairly large small group, as you just need to give them this tip and set them to work. Or you could bring together just two kids, quickly teach them this concept and get them to practice it so they "own it," and then you can set *them* up to teach others.

For students who struggle to find motifs or to develop themes that are more than one word, it may help to coach them to first come up with more powerful or provocative single words, by asking, "What troubles are hiding in this text?" and providing or co-creating a kind of trouble wall, or chart, with possibilities.

SHARE

Considering Themes that Arise in Genres, Series, and in Works by Certain Authors

Readers can think about how some themes come up in books in certain genres, series, or in books by specific authors.

"Readers, I know when you were younger, you probably looked at some themes that were true in more than one book. Well, it can also be interesting to look at how certain kinds of themes come up in certain genres and authors. For instance, in historical fiction, readers might often find a theme like, 'Children grow up rapidly in times of violence.' In the same way, in fantasy novels, a theme like 'Even ordinary people can be heroes' often arises.

"So right now, will you sort yourselves into small groups, getting together with others who are reading the same genres? Or maybe the same authors or series? Do some thinking about if there are certain kinds of themes that tend to come up in your books."

SESSION 17 HOMEWORK

 EVALUATING THE SIGNIFICANCE OF THEMES

After you've read tonight for about forty minutes, and thirty to forty pages, think about the themes in your novel. Remember, you can start thinking about possible themes early in the book—you don't have to wait till the end. Think, "Perhaps this is about . . ." or "The story might be teaching readers that . . ." Weigh and evaluate which themes seem most important in your novel. You could consider, for instance, which themes might be truer across more of the story. Or you might think about which ones might matter in your life, or in the world. Then choose one theme that seems particularly significant. Take a few minutes to think about that theme and write a bit in your notebook about why that theme matters. Explain what seems important about it.

SESSION 17: MOVING FROM MOTIFS TO THEMES

Session 18

Investigating How Symbolism Relates to Themes

GETTING READY

- Prepare to display cards from "Narrative Writers Use Techniques Such As . . ." chart (see Connection). 👆

- Write a theme sentence on a large sticky note and be ready to display it (see Teaching).

- Prepare to show part of the Taylor Swift video, "You Belong with Me," where the girl dances in her bedroom. A link to the video is available in the online resources (see Teaching). 👆

- Prepare to display the "Narrative Writers Aim Toward Goals Such As . . ." chart (see Teaching). 👆

- Display and add to Bend III anchor chart, "To Investigate Themes . . ." (see Link). 👆

IN THIS SESSION

TODAY YOU'LL teach students that authors often layer symbolism in narratives, and that these symbols are often related to significant themes. Readers consider how symbols relate to or develop an important theme.

TODAY YOUR STUDENTS may continue the work of tracing motifs and investigating themes, alongside the new work of investigating symbols as another way to explore theme. If they are just starting a book, some may be doing character and setting work first. As always, students should have Post-its and notebooks at the ready as they read, and they should plan for what they want to talk about with their partner, and for their ongoing work.

MINILESSON

CONNECTION

Remind students of the work they've been doing, and introduce analyzing symbolism as the next step in this exploration.

"Readers, I've been thinking about you, and the work you've been doing. In fact, I've been telling colleagues about some of the themes you are discovering, because you're making me see new things in these books. Like, I read *The Maze Runner* a couple of times and watched the movie, and I never thought about how maybe it suggests that having special gifts can be a torment, because people want to use you.

142

"It's really cool that you're coming up with lots of themes for each novel. A totally different theme for *The Maze Runner*, that I also never thought of before, was that special gifts can be a blessing, because you can use them to help others. So interesting! You're making me want to read a lot of these books again.

"You're also making me want to study *how* these authors develop these themes, because I suspect they are doing more than simply using the plot. I bet they are using some interesting craft moves as well." I held up a set of cards labeled "Narrative Writers Use Techniques Such As . . . ," which some students remembered from writing workshop. "Glance at these narrative techniques with your partner—you may have seen them before in writing workshop. Is there a technique here that you've seen your author use?"

I gave students a moment to talk, and then called them back.

"Readers, I hear you talking about how some authors use flashback, while others use multiple plotlines, and others particularly change the tone a lot. And some of you talked about symbolism. I'd like to explore that further today, because symbolism often is deeply related to theme."

Visual checklists help students both find more techniques in the texts they are reading and find academic language to describe these techniques.

❖ **Name the teaching point.**

"Today I want to teach you that once you have an idea for a theme in the story, you can look to see whether the author has written the story in a way that advances that theme. One way to do this is to search for symbolism—objects or moments that take on special significance and help develop the theme."

TEACHING

Return to a theme you developed yesterday. First, name a series of steps readers use to think about themes, and then to find moments that support that theme, to investigate with a craft lens.

"Watch me do this work. As you watch, think about the parts of this work that you're already good at, and the parts that might be tricky. One way I do this work is first, I think about themes I've discovered in my story, like we did yesterday. I focus on a theme that I'm particularly interested in. I'm fascinated by the theme we considered in 'You Belong with Me,' for instance." I put up a large Post-it with the theme:

> It's hard to be yourself.

SESSION 18: INVESTIGATING HOW SYMBOLISM RELATES TO THEMES

"Second, I think back over the story, to moments that supported this theme. We did some of this yesterday, so think with me . . . it felt like we saw this theme in a few moments, including when the girl seems to struggle to figure out who she is, when being herself seems to make her invisible, and when she changes herself for love, or to fit in."

"Then third, I go back to these moments, and I investigate if the author used any interesting craft there—in this case, did the author use any possible symbolism? This is the part that gets tricky . . . and interesting."

Doing a kind of shared reading, revisit parts of the video "text" to investigate author's craft, particularly symbolism.

I pulled up the part of the video where the girl dances in her bedroom. "Let's do this together. We'll 'reread' together. We're looking for possible symbolism that might relate to this theme. Hmm, . . . so there are all her different clothes . . . and there's stuff on the walls . . . Let's see, there are books, and a big poster of . . ." I paused the video. "Hey! It's a huge butterfly opening its wings! Hmm! Do you agree that the butterfly has symbolic possibilities?" I looked around. "Talk to a partner. What is it making you think?"

I listened in as students talked avidly about the butterfly and possible symbolism, with ideas ranging from it being beautiful, to being short-lived, to being fragile, to being an insect that changes itself drastically inside a cocoon. Then I called them back.

"So we agree that this butterfly, right in the middle of her wall, feels symbolic, and there are different possibilities for *how* it is symbolic. We're looking to relate it to our theme and to explain how it might help develop the theme. Our explanation doesn't have to be perfect. It just needs to help us think about how symbolism and theme might work together.

"See what you think of this explanation . . . I'm using some of what I was thinking and some of what you were thinking." I pointed to the girl spinning around in her handmade clothes, and the butterfly image behind her. "Here, it's as if the girl is just a caterpillar, spinning and making herself. But all the time, she could become a beautiful butterfly." I fast-forwarded to the end. "And at the end . . . she's really become the butterfly, now she's beautiful, or at least what some people would call beautiful.

"So maybe . . . one way the author shows that the girl struggles with being herself is by suggesting that she might be like a butterfly—sort of ugly at first, but all the time capable of becoming beautiful. I'm not sure I *like* that message, but I think it's there. Remember, this was one of the themes we came to by thinking about hidden messages."

Recap how readers revisit important parts of the story and consider possible symbolism.

"Readers, did you see how we returned to places in the story that suggested a theme, and we investigated possible symbolism? And then we explored ways this symbolism might help develop that theme? And it led us to some new thinking?"

ACTIVE ENGAGEMENT

Give students a chance to try this work in their own books. First, give them an additional tip, to start with places where the reader sees symbolism and consider possible thematic connections.

"In a moment, you'll have a chance to try this work. Here's one tip. Another way to do this work would be to start with symbols, and see if they suggest themes, including ones you've thought of already, or perhaps new ones.

"For example, if I started by thinking about the butterfly as a symbol, it makes me want to investigate another possible theme—'Some people want girls to be like butterflies, special only for their beauty.' Or I could start with another symbol in our video text, the girl's glasses for example. I think we could come up with a lot of ideas about the symbolism of those, and how that might relate to a theme.

"Think about your own books. Are there any parts in your stories that feel symbolic, that might support an interesting theme? Take a minute to think, and *definitely* go back to a specific passage. When you have an idea, give your partner a nod, and share your thinking."

I gave partners a moment to try this work out.

LINK

Recap. Then invite students to add this work to their repertoires.

"Readers, this is fascinating work. I'm guessing that many of the books you're reading are full of symbolism, and perhaps other techniques you see on this chart. Challenge yourself to explore not only what themes a story suggests, but how the author develops these themes. I'll be curious to see how you use your notebook to capture some of this thinking. Some of you particularly notice images, so making small sketches might help you to think.

"I'll add this work to our anchor chart, and you add it to your repertoire. Now take a quick moment to talk to your partner about the work you'll do today, before you go off."

ANCHOR CHART

To Investigate Themes . . .

- Consider how characters' conflicts become motifs.
- Ask what the author has to say about a motif.
  - Question the text.
  - Develop possible theme statements.
- **Notice possible symbolism, and think about how it relates to themes.**

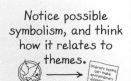

Notice possible symbolism, and think how it relates to themes.

CONFERRING AND SMALL-GROUP WORK

Learning More about Students' Reading Lives

YOUR STUDENTS HAVE A LOT OF WORK they can be doing as readers. They should, by now, be on their third or fourth book, with your lower-level readers reading several more, as those books are shorter and easier. Meanwhile, you will always want to be checking in with students about their reading lives. Find out how much they are reading, how they are fitting reading in, what they are reading, and what work they are doing as readers. It's daunting, when you may have anywhere from sixty to a hundred readers to keep track of. At the same time, this is the thing you teach. Helping your students to take charge of their reading is invaluable instruction that will extend beyond this class and this year.

One tip is that you don't always have to do your research and instruction on the same day. Take time to find out about students' reading lives, and then plan strategic small groups or partner work, based on what you find out, for tomorrow and beyond. Tomorrow's conferring and small-group work can tackle "fix-it" strategies and methods to support kids. Today, you're researching. Here's what this might look like.

Finding Out About Volume, Book Choice, Time Spent Reading

To conduct this research, you might ask students to have their reading logs out, and then pull up alongside individual kids and invite them to give you a tour of their reading lives so far. Ask them to explain what books they've been reading and why. Look closely at how many books they've read, how many pages they seem to read, and what days they are reading more or less. Look for what kinds of books seem to get them reading more or less. Give major compliments for honesty and integrity. You can only help students if they are open about what's hard. They can only grow if they are honest about where they struggle.

Finding Out What Gets in the Way of Reading

If you see signs of low reading volume, on the log or simply by finding out what kids have read so far, try to find out more about what is getting in the way of reading. Find out if these students are reading right before bed, at the end of homework, or when. Find out what other responsibilities and activities they have. Find out how much sleep they are getting. Think about if any of the books they are holding are too hard, or not relatable or engaging enough. Ask what kinds of movies and television shows they like, and if they ever struggle to stay awake during those. Find out where they try to read, and how quiet it is, and comfortable. See if there is any day of the week when they may have more open time.

Finding Mentors and Problem Solvers

You'll also want to look for students who are becoming more avid readers. These students will be good mentors for others. Look for students whose logs show increases in pages read or smarter book choices. Look for kids who are buying books or getting them from libraries or friends. Look for kids who are finding series and genres and sticking to them. Look for students who are reading in more than one language, and finding books in each. Look, as well, at how readers are using their reading notebooks, how they are using Post-its or annotating, and keep track of student work that seems to reflect the thinking work you are teaching in class. All these students will have potential to mentor others.

As you move around today, use your compassion and honesty to consider how hard it is to be a preteen or teen, how complicated their lives are. Compliment them on how they are beginning to manage these lives and reflect on them. Talk a bit about the books they are reading. Make the experience quick and engaging. Let your students know that as they research their books, you are researching them, so that you can help them become more powerful readers.

SHARE

Partners Reflect on Their Reading Lives

Encourage readers to reflect with a partner on what's going well and what's still challenging for them as readers.

"Readers, you've done some interesting work today. It's also important to think about the bigger picture of your reading—how much reading you're getting done, how you're choosing books, how your writing about reading is becoming both more efficient and more purposeful, and now, perhaps more artful. Can you reflect for a moment with your partner about what's going well in reading, and how you're growing? If there are challenges, talk about those with your partner as well, and we'll do some work tomorrow together around those challenges."

SESSION 18 HOMEWORK

 ### READING FOR SYMBOLS

Readers, today and across this unit, you've shifted into being a different kind of readers. You aren't readers who read just to find out what happens in a book. You are readers who pause, who reflect, and who know that most everything in a book has deeper meaning. Tonight as you read, pay particular attention to possible symbols in your novels. Notice what characters wear and carry, consider weather and setting details, pay attention to what characters remember and notice. Let these details push you to think more deeply about themes that are emerging in your book. Also strive to attain your reading goals tonight—read for at least forty minutes and get through thirty to forty pages.

Session 19

Taking Charge of Your Collaborative Reading Life

GETTING READY

✓ Display and add to chart, "What's Most Worth Working on Together?" (see Teaching).

✓ Make sure students can reference anchor charts, "To Think Deeply about Characters..." (Bend I), "To Investigate the Influence of Setting on Characters..." (Bend II), and "To Investigate Themes..." (Bend III) (see Link).

IN THIS SESSION

TODAY YOU'LL teach students that partners can take charge of their collaborative reading lives by considering what's worth working on together, then making sure their writing about reading and talk reflect that focus. You'll teach students to lean on each other, support each other, and push each other.

TODAY YOUR STUDENTS will plan the work they will do with their partner, developing specific ideas on what to work on together and how to get those things done effectively. During the share, partners will put their study plans they developed during the minilesson into action.

MINILESSON

CONNECTION

Explain that up to this point in the unit, you have channeled partners to work together in fairly prescribed ways. Rally students to take charge of their reading lives, and to work together.

"Readers, up to this point in the unit, we've been having partner shares where often I gave you pointers about work you could do with your partner or other readers.

"Before this unit is over, I want to remind you of something that you have learned before, over the years. And that is that the real goal is for you to have all these optional strategies, all these ways of reading, and for you to draw on them in ways that make sense, as you read. The real goal is for you to not need a teacher reminding you that everything you have learned in this unit is meant as a strategy for life."

❖ **Name the teaching point.**

"Today I want to remind you that readers take charge of their work time, including the work they do together. They mull over options, and then ask themselves, 'What's most worth thinking about?' Then, they design their work together."

TEACHING

Walk students through a handful of ways reading partners can work together during collaborative time. Set them up to make smart choices for their partnership.

"Can I walk you through some of the things you and your partner might think and talk about together? As I talk about each one, consider whether that choice might make sense for you and your partner today."

I revealed a new chart, "What's Most Worth Working on Together?"

"Sometimes, you'll need to talk about how your reading is going—what genres you've been reading, how long you've been reading, what books are getting you to read more, things like that. If this is the case, you can decide to study your reading logs together, poring over them to notice patterns and set goals." I added "Use your reading logs to study your reading lives" to the chart.

"Other times, things won't be going so well. Maybe you're having trouble staying focused on your reading, or maybe you're reading a new book and it just doesn't make any sense. Maybe you've started a new sport season, and you're just . . . tired. You might bring that problem to your partner and ask questions, talk about the problem, and brainstorm possible solutions." I gestured to the chart.

"Most of the time, you'll probably be talking about the reading work you're doing and the new ideas that reading work leads you to. Maybe you paid attention to how the setting was affecting the characters or how characters were revealed slowly. Or maybe you've been finding motifs, or you've been fascinated by symbolism. You could bring that information to your partnership and talk a lot about it." I added to the chart "Talk about the reading work you did and the new ideas it led you to."

"Especially if you and your partner are reading the same book, you might decide on one idea or a few ideas to track as you read. You could both read with those ideas in mind, collecting a lot of thoughts related to those ideas. Then, when you meet, you could share what you noticed and discuss your new thoughts." I wrote, "Decide on an idea to track, and discuss your new thoughts about that idea."

"And finally, even if you're not reading the same book, you might decide on a shared motif, symbols, or theme, to see how it plays out in different books." I added this to the chart.

What's Most Worth Working on Together?

* Use your reading logs to study your reading lives.

* Bring problems to the conversation and brainstorm solutions.

* Talk about the reading work you did and the new ideas it led you to.

* Decide on an idea to track, and discuss your new thoughts about that idea.

* Trace shared motifs, symbols, or themes across different models.

* Design your own focus!

Explain that students can also develop their own ways to work together. Reveal the completed partner chart.

"Those are just some ideas. You and your partner might develop something else you think is most worth working on together. I'll leave a few blank Post-its at the bottom so you can add your own ideas." I added the final point and stuck a few blank Post-its to the chart.

ACTIVE ENGAGEMENT

Channel partners to consider how they will spend their partner time, weighing different options to determine which will be most beneficial.

"Partners, it's all up to you. Will you work with your partner to determine how best to develop your partner time? Ask, 'What's most worth working on together?' Propose a possibility and then discuss if that's what's most important right now for your reading life. Talk until you come to a consensus."

While students worked, I coached in and voiced over with tips:

- "Don't just decide on the first possibility you name. Try out a few to figure out what will *most* be worth working on today."

- "Maybe you can decide on a focus for more than one day—that is, work you could develop over a few days."

- "You decided to track an idea. Talk together about which idea(s) might most be worth tracking."

- "If you're designing your own focus, name it clearly so that you and your partner are both on the same page about the work you're doing."

Encourage partners to develop a plan for what they need to prepare and how they'll use their time.

"Once you know what you want to talk about, develop a plan with your partner. What will you need to do to prepare for your conversation? How will you make the most of your time together?" I gave students a minute to brainstorm.

Share out the plans a few partnerships developed.

"You're developing plans that will really help you take charge of your collaborative work time. One partnership decided to track a big idea. They decided to both pay particular attention to how characters are affected by the setting. They agreed to jot a little about it, so they'll be ready to talk at the end of reading workshop today. Another partnership

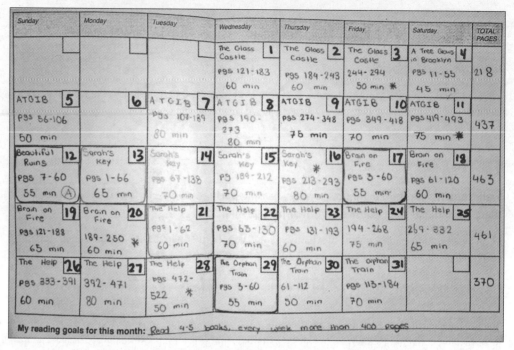

FIG. 19–1 Chloe uses her log to reflect and set goals. She's serious about her reading.

decided to divide up the two main characters in their book. Today, they'll each pay special attention to one of those characters as they read and then they'll compare their findings. These are really purposeful reading plans."

LINK

Send students off with a reminder to keep the plan they made with their partner in mind while reading. Revisit earlier anchor charts so students remember to draw on a repertoire of work.

"Readers, as you head off to read today, keep the study plan you made with your partner in mind. You might do some thinking work or jotting to get yourself ready for partner time." I gestured toward our earlier anchor charts, "To Think Deeply about Characters . . ." (Bend I) and "To Investigate the Influence of Setting on Characters . . ." (Bend II) and said, "Some of this work is probably becoming automatic for you. If so, make sure you are challenging yourself, perhaps by doing more of this new work." I motioned to our new chart, "To Investigate Themes . . ." (Bend III).

"Off you go!"

CONFERRING AND SMALL-GROUP WORK

Following Up on Students' Reading Lives

YESTERDAY, you did a lot of research, visiting with students to find out more about their reading lives, from how much they are reading to the kind of reading work they are doing. Today, you can apply what you learned to some strategic small groups, partnership work, and individual conferences.

Advising Strong and Avid Readers—Building Social Coalition

You'll undoubtedly have discovered among your students some strong and avid readers—kids who read for long stretches of time, carry books everywhere, and could seemingly fall into the category of "don't need you." But they *do* need you. It's not so easy to be a secret geek or an open nerd in middle and high school. In his study, *City Schools and the American Dream*, Pedro Noguera talks about how important it is to make it cool to be smart. If peer culture and academic culture don't coincide, Noguera warns, peer culture will always win. You might, therefore, gather these avid readers and help them form small social groups around reading. Say explicitly that these readers are powerful and have the potential to become even more powerful. Suggest that they begin to choose books together, and even courses of study. Suggest that they meet outside of class, virtually or in person. Also, make book suggestions. These readers may be ready for more adult levels of text complexity. Think about the authors whom adults around the world read and offer some suggestions for a book club. Mostly, create a vision for these students of building coalition, social bonds, and academic capital together.

Never, Ever Give Up on Helping Kids Get More Reading Done—Fitting Reading into Complicated Lives

You'll also find some students who, even with the best intentions, are struggling to fit reading into their lives. You are likely aware of many of their responsibilities through your research into their reading lives. Adolescents often have grown-up responsibilities and commitments—caring for siblings, doing the bookkeeping for a family business, playing midfield on multiple soccer teams. The whole enterprise of managing school, family, friends, and life is often overwhelming to preteens and teens.

To support these kids, sit with one or two at a time, and think of what you are doing as a kind of intervention, where you are going to look at every possibility for how to fit in more reading. I remember sitting with a sixth-grader in Brooklyn, who ultimately decided that every Sunday, when she sat for two hours getting her hair done (a tradition with the women in her family), was when she would read. Another student, who had to watch siblings in the evening, needed a home visit to explain the significance of reading, and to think together with the family about how to fit in some reading time. Each case is personal. If you make it personal, kids who weren't reading begin to read.

Embracing Seemingly Disengaged Nonreaders

Some of your students present a front that makes it seem as if they just don't care. They don't like reading, they say, or they're bored. It can be frustrating and saddening and disempowering as a teacher, when you want to offer all you have, and children don't seem to want anything. Hang in there. This has happened to all of us, it will happen again, and there is no miracle cure.

Some advice: when kids say "I don't like something," it's code for, "I find this hard." So one approach may be to seek out an experienced reading specialist (ideally a Reading Recovery specialist) and find out more about what is going on with this reader. There may be something going on that a reading specialist or a primary reading teacher (if you have one in your building) may be able to help you assess. Another approach is to find out if a student's life outside of school may make school seem less important right now. Find out what the child is writing about in writing workshop. Talk a bit about what his or her days and weekends are like. Love him or her up. You can't discipline a kid into being a reader. But sometimes, you can love him or her into it. And mostly, follow up. If you recommend a new book, text later, "How's it going? Did you try the book?" If a student promises to read over the weekend, show how you are setting an alert on your calendar to text on Sunday, with a good luck text.

One last tip. Sometimes reluctant students respond more to peers than to teachers. Enlist students from upper grades to come in and run some peer conferring groups.

Ruthlessly take advantage of social capital. Get those cool kids in. Often kids who seem to barely engage with an adult teacher suddenly lean forward and listen when an older teen teaches them, especially one whom they admire.

SHARE

Rallying Partners to Talk in Self-Selected Ways

Suggest ways for students to prepare to make the most of their partner time.

"It's almost time to get together with your partner. Remember that today, you and your partner are in charge of your talk time. Before you meet with your partner, will you take a minute or two to prepare? You might look over what you read and flag an important part or two to talk about. Or jot a few quick notes about major points you want to raise. You might even mull over a problem you're having and think about how to describe what's tricky to your partner so you can get the help you need. Use this time right now to get yourself ready."

I gave students a minute or two to prepare while I moved from table to table, offering quick words of encouragement.

Then I invited students to work with their partners. "You're in charge. Get with your partner, and put your study plan into action. Make the most of the time you have together!"

SESSION 19 HOMEWORK

 FOLLOWING UP ON PARTNERSHIP WORK

Readers, tonight, use the work you are doing with your partner to push yourself to read differently. Do this in two ways. First, follow up on the thinking from your conversation in class today. Continue to search for evidence to support or refute some of the points you and your partner discussed. And second, gather fresh ideas that you think would make for good partner talk. Be sure to record these so you are prepared for your next conversation. As always, read for at least forty minutes tonight and aim to read at least thirty to forty pages.

Session 20

Read-Aloud
Reading Aloud to Support Repertoire and Agency

IN THIS SESSION

TODAY YOU'LL encourage readers to make choices and draw flexibly on a range of reading skills during a read-aloud of "Thank You, M'am" by Langston Hughes.

TODAY AS YOUR STUDENTS participate in the read-aloud and as they read their own books, they will strike a balance between metacognitive reflection and deepening their reading skills, as they notice and name the reading work called for in different parts of the book.

GETTING READY

- Prepare these items before you teach today: Write a Post-it, "What thinking work does this text want us to do?" Be ready to put it at the top of blank chart paper. From anchor charts, choose the reading work your students have been most interested in. Write these points, worded slightly differently from the charts, on large Post-its (different colors). Have smaller blank Post-its to write students' ideas for reading work and to put them on chart paper (see Connection and Conducting the Read-Aloud).

- Prepare to read aloud from "Thank You, M'am" by Langston Hughes (see Conducting the Read-Aloud).

- Make anchor charts available to students: "To Think Deeply about Characters . . ." (Bend I), "To Investigate the Influence of Setting on Characters . . ." (Bend II), and "To Investigate Themes . . ." (Bend III) (see Connection).

- You may want to take a photo of your class's reading work chart (see Link).

- Provide students with Post-its and markers (see Independent Reading).

- You may wish to refer to chart, "'Lean in' Comments to Build Student Energy for Independent Thinking," as you work with students (see Independent Reading).

CONNECTION

Introduce students to the concept of a repertoire read-aloud by sharing a sports analogy.

"Readers, we've done a few read-alouds together these last few weeks, and so far, I've often been the one calling the shots. I've often picked where we'll stop and decided what we should talk about at those points.

"Here's the thing. I think our read-alouds so far have been a lot like the drills you do in soccer practice, where the coach has you practice passing the ball back and forth for twenty minutes. Your skills get better, but someone else is giving you directions.

"Today, I thought we could all get in the game. You know how when you're in a soccer game, the coach can't say, 'Dribble!' 'Shoot!' 'Pass!' You have to do that. You have to be the one to call the shots.

"Reading on your own is like a soccer game. In a game, you have to read what's going on, and decide what to do next. When you read on your own, no one is there to tell you what to think about. You have to decide, based on what's going on in the story.

"Today we'll try a repertoire read-aloud, where you'll call the shots. I won't tell you what to think about as you listen. Instead, you'll have to ask, 'What thinking work does this text want us to do?'" I posted the question on a big Post-it on a piece of blank chart paper. "Chances are, if you're alert, the text will almost suggest the kinds of thinking work that make sense. Maybe the author will spend a whole paragraph building a mood, and you'll know to stop and ask, 'What kind of place is this?'"

Channel students to study the anchor charts from Bends I, II, and III to recall common thinking work readers do as they read.

"You've done a lot of reading work that is captured on our anchor charts." I gestured toward our charts. "I've taken some of the most fascinating points and put them on large Post-its. You'll see I worded them a bit differently from our anchor charts to make them shorter and to reflect the reading work I've seen you most interested in over the last few weeks."

I had arranged these large different-colored Post-its on the left side of a piece of chart paper. "Take a moment and look at these and talk to a partner. Which of these have you been doing more of?"

CONDUCTING THE READ-ALOUD

Read aloud the first section of the text. Rally students to listen, asking, "What thinking work does this text want us to do?" Then provide time for partners to talk.

"Ready to give this a try? I've included some blank Post-its as well, because it's possible you'll try some new reading work. You might think the story is pushing you in a direction we haven't gone yet in our reading.

"I'm going to read aloud a new text, 'Thank You, M'am' by Langston Hughes. Your job is to call the shots." On a chart I had jotted our inquiry question, "What thinking work does this text want us to do?" I gestured to the chart and said, "Keep this question in mind as we read. Be ready to share your thinking when I pause."

FIG. 20–1 Chart paper with optional reading work on large Post-its, before the read-aloud

> **Thank You, M'am**
> by Langston Hughes
>
> She was a large woman with a large purse that had everything in it but a hammer and nails. It had a long strap, and she carried it slung across her shoulder. It was about eleven o'clock at night, dark, and she was walking alone, when a boy ran up behind her and tried to snatch her purse. The strap broke with the sudden single tug the boy gave it from behind. But the boy's weight and the weight of the purse combined caused him to lose his balance. Instead of taking off full blast as he had hoped, the boy fell on his back on the sidewalk and his legs flew up. The large woman simply turned around and kicked him right square in his blue-jeaned sitter. Then she reached down, picked the boy up by his shirt front, and shook him until his teeth rattled.
>
> After that the woman said, "Pick up my pocketbook, boy, and give it here."

"Go ahead, tell your partner. What are you thinking? What's most interesting here?"

Translate what students talk about into replicable work. Use the large Post-its as manipulatives to chart the reading work that students do, and use smaller Post-its to record new work.

As students talked, I listened for reading work named on our large Post-its, and prepared to jot on smaller Post-its the new work I heard them trying.

One partnership noted how surprised they were when the woman kicked the boy, and talked about how unusually tough she seemed. I said, "Readers, I heard some of you noting what the old woman does in the story, and talking about her character traits, especially how unusually tough she seems." I moved the larger Post-it, "Noticing details that suggest character traits," to the middle of the chart, to show that was work the students were doing.

On a smaller Post-it, I jotted "Noting unusual traits." I attached this smaller one to the larger Post-it I had just moved to suggest this was a new way they were extending the work.

| Noticing details that suggest character traits | Noting unusual traits |

There is something about moving these Post-its as kids do the reading work, and filling in blank Post-its with the reading work kids invent, that energizes students. Your kids will talk about details in the text. You name it as reading work. So, when you ask, "What reading work do you want to do now? What's fascinating here?," they'll talk for instance about how the boy isn't able to wrestle the handbag from the old woman. You say, "Oh, you're talking about characters who are surprisingly strong. So interesting. I bet you mean strong inside and outside!"

I continued, "I heard others talking about how the boy made a bad move and got caught. One partnership was wondering what the boy would have done if he had successfully grabbed her purse. They wondered if he is someone who always steals, or if he has other sides, too. They even talked about what might have caused him to steal." I moved the larger Post-it, "Recognizing less likeable sides of characters," to the center of the chart. "We might also add some new work, 'Empathizing with characters, even when we don't agree with their choices.'" I wrote this on a smaller Post-it and added it to the larger Post-it I had just moved.

"I also heard a partnership talking about how this scene is happening at night. The darkness makes this scene feel all the more ominous." I moved the Post-it "Recognizing when/how the setting becomes significant" to the center of the chart.

"Nice work. Let's go on. Now it's like you're really in the scrimmage."

I reread a bit, and then read on.

> . . . right square in his blue-jeaned sitter. Then she reached down, picked the boy up by his shirt front, and shook him until his teeth rattled.
>
> After that the woman said, "Pick up my pocketbook, boy, and give it here."
>
> She still held him tightly. But she bent down enough to permit him to stoop and pick up her purse. Then she said, "Now ain't you ashamed of yourself?"
>
> Firmly gripped by his shirt front, the boy said, "Yes'm."
>
> The woman said, "What did you want to do it for?"
>
> The boy said, "I didn't aim to."
>
> She said, "You a lie!"
>
> By that time two or three people passed, stopped, turned to look, and some stood watching.
>
> "If I turn you loose, will you run?" asked the woman.
>
> "Yes'm," said the boy.
>
> "Then I won't turn you loose," said the woman. She did not release him.
>
> "Lady, I'm sorry," whispered the boy.
>
> "Um-hum! Your face is dirty. I got a great mind to wash your face for you. Ain't you got nobody home to tell you to wash your face?"
>
> "No'm," said the boy.
>
> "Then it will get washed this evening," said the large woman starting up the street, dragging the frightened boy behind her.

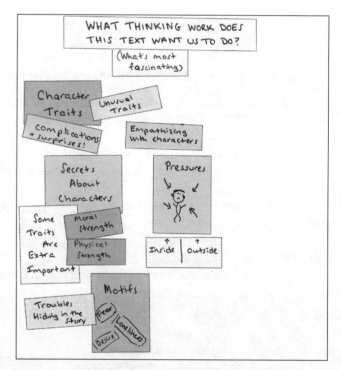

FIG. 20–2 The chart partway through the read-aloud

Channel partners to turn and talk. Do your best to name what students do and make it seem like intriguing and innovative thinking work.

"So interesting! What did you find most interesting? What are you figuring out?"

I listened as students talked about how complicated the characters were, how surprising that the boy was honest, and how surprising it was that the woman wanted to help him rather than call the police. I jotted as they wrote, again, trying my best to turn what they were saying into replicable reading work.

"I heard you naming details from the story to talk about how complicated these characters are. You also talked about how these characters are surprising—they don't act the way we expect them to. Let's add both to our chart. We already have our 'Noticing details that suggest character traits' Post-it in the middle, but I think we can add on to that." I jotted "Recognizing characters are complicated," on a small Post-it, and on another, "Letting characters surprise us." I attached them to the large character Post-it.

Rally students to try similar types of thinking work and new thinking work as you read on.

"Let's go on. I'm curious if you'll find yourself deepening some of this thinking work, or if the text will push you in new directions." I gestured at our inquiry question, "What kind of thinking work does this text want us to do?" Then I reread a bit and read on.

"Then it will get washed this evening," said the large woman starting up the street, dragging the frightened boy behind her.

He looked as if he were fourteen or fifteen, frail and willow-wild, in tennis shoes and blue jeans.

The woman said, "You ought to be my son. I would teach you right from wrong. Least I can do right now is to wash your face. Are you hungry?"

"No'm," said the being dragged boy. "I just want you to turn me loose."

"Was I bothering *you* when I turned that corner?" asked the woman.

"No'm."

"But you put yourself in contact with *me*," said the woman. "If you think that that contact is not going to last awhile, you got another thought coming. When I get through with you, sir, you are going to remember Mrs. Luella Bates Washington Jones."

Sweat popped out on the boy's face and he began to struggle. Mrs. Jones stopped, jerked him around in front of her, put a half-nelson about his neck, and continued to drag him up the street. When she got to her door, she dragged the boy inside, down a hall, and into a large kitchenette-furnished room at the rear of the house. She switched on the light and left the door open. The boy could hear other roomers laughing and talking in the large house. Some of their doors were open, too, so he knew he and the woman were not alone. The woman still had him by the neck in the middle of her room.

I paused my reading, and said to students, "What do you think!? Turn and talk."

Name out the thinking work readers did, retelling some of the details, then pausing to invite them to help you name any work that is complicated. Then, read aloud another section of the text.

This time, as students talked, I moved over the Post-it for "Realizing some traits become extra important." Then I said, "I can hear almost all of you talking about how strong this woman is, and how it helps her take charge of this boy. It's that thing, where some character traits turn out to be more important than others in the story. I feel like you're also talking about two kinds of strength though—her physical and her moral strength. What should we call that? What do you think?"

I listened to partners murmur to each other, and said, "Hmm, . . . it sounds like you are saying that perhaps we should list up here, 'Noting characters' internal and external strengths (and weaknesses).' Let's add that. Very interesting." I wrote this on a small Post-it, and connected it to the large Post-it I had just moved.

Invite readers to think about any reading work they haven't done. Read on, inviting them to remain alert for places the text calls for this remaining work.

"Readers, before we go on, it might be worth it to look at the reading work we haven't done yet, and consider if any of this might pay off. Let's look for a moment." We looked at what remained on the left side of the chart.

"Let's go on. Keep in mind what we haven't talked about yet. I'm wondering, for example, are we considering the psychology or mood of the setting and how it changes? Maybe we should rethink that first scene as compared to the later scenes. I'm also thinking that it might be helpful to consider conflicts that are hiding in this story, and see if any become motifs." I gestured to the chart. "In any case, let's keep these in mind."

I continued reading.

She said, "What is your name?"

"Roger," answered the boy.

"Then, Roger, you go to that sink and wash your face," said the woman, whereupon she turned him loose—at last. Roger looked at the door—looked at the woman—looked at the door—*and went to the sink*.

"Let the water run until it gets warm," she said. "Here's a clean towel."

"You gonna take me to jail?" asked the boy, bending over the sink.

"Not with that face, I would not take you nowhere," said the woman. "Here I am trying to get home to cook me a bite to eat and you snatch my pocketbook! Maybe, you ain't been to your supper either, late as it be. Have you?"

"There's nobody home at my house," said the boy.

"Then we'll eat," said the woman. "I believe you're hungry—or been hungry—to try to snatch my pocketbook."

"I want a pair of blue suede shoes," said the boy.

> "Well, you didn't have to snatch *my* pocketbook to get some suede shoes," said Mrs. Luella Bates Washington Jones. "You could of asked me."
>
> "M'am?"
>
> The water dripping from his face, the boy looked at her. There was a long pause. A very long pause. After he had dried his face, and not knowing what else to do, dried it again, the boy turned around, wondering what next. The door was open. He could make a dash for it down the hall. He could run, run, run, *run!*
>
> The woman was sitting on the daybed. After a while she said, "I were young once and I wanted things I could not get."
>
> There was another long pause. The boy's mouth opened. Then he frowned, not knowing he frowned.
>
> The woman said, "Um-hum! You thought I was going to say *but*, didn't you? You thought I was going to say, *but I didn't snatch people's pocketbooks*. Well, I wasn't going to say that." Pause. Silence. "I have done things, too, which I would not tell you, son—neither tell God, if He didn't already know. So you set down while I fix us something to eat. You might run that comb through your hair so you will look presentable."
>
> In another corner of the room behind a screen was a gas plate and an icebox. Mrs. Jones got up and went behind the screen. The woman did not watch the boy to see if he was going to run now, nor did she watch her purse which she left behind her on the daybed. But the boy took care to sit on the far side of the room, away from the purse, where he thought she could easily see him out of the corner of her eye, if she wanted to. He did not trust the woman *not* to trust him. And he did not want to be mistrusted now.
>
> "Do you need somebody to go to the store," asked the boy, "maybe to get some milk or something?"
>
> "Don't believe I do," said the woman, "unless you just want sweet milk yourself. I was going to make cocoa out of this canned milk I got here."
>
> "That will be fine," said the boy.

Channel students to talk, and listen, poised to learn about what your students are good at and what they are only beginning to think about. Keep up their energy by naming their reading work, and help with some language to elevate their thinking as needed.

"I can see you have a lot to say. Go ahead, what are you thinking?"

After a few minutes, I said, "I heard some of you talking about lessons this boy might be learning." I moved the big Post-it, "Considering lessons characters learn," to the center of the chart. "You talked about how he is learning that kindness goes a lot farther than stealing. And how trust is something precious, that has to be earned."

I gestured for students to continue talking. One partnership said, "I'm noticing that sometimes the author is using the characters' names and sometimes he's not. That seems kind of weird. Most authors just use the characters' names all the time. I wonder why he's doing that." Others talked about how the boy seems to change across the story. Many talked about the issue of poverty that seems to run through the story.

"Readers, you just did a lot of reading work." I moved over the Post-its, "Recognizing troubles hiding in the story" and "Thinking about motifs." "You talked about how motifs like poverty and hardship and hunger seem to run through this story. You were on the edge of talking about themes as well. I'll jot some of those so you can keep them in mind as we read on." On small Post-its, I jotted "People can change," "Poverty can make people hard," and "Goodness is contagious," up near the big Post-it, "Considering possible themes," to help students to crystallize their ideas.

I continued, "Readers, two students just invented a new kind of reading work that we have to add to our chart. They noticed an author's craft move—that the author sometimes uses character names and sometimes doesn't—and they pushed themselves to consider why the author might have done that. I added, "Notice author's craft" to the chart. I wrote this on a large Post-it to show it was different from the other thinking work.

Set students up to listen as you read aloud the last section of the text. Name any transferable reading work that students invent, and add it to the chart.

"Readers, we've just got one more section to read. Keep thinking, 'What reading work does this part want us to do?' It might be the reading work that's on the chart, or you might develop some of your own reading work."

> She heated some lima beans and ham she had in the icebox, made the cocoa, and set the table. The woman did not ask the boy anything about where he lived, or his folks, or anything else that would embarrass him. Instead, as they ate, she told him about her job in a hotel beauty-shop that stayed open late, what the work was like, and how all kinds of women came in and out, blondes, red-heads, and Spanish. Then she cut him a half of her ten-cent cake.
>
> "Eat some more, son," she said.
>
> When they were finished eating she got up and said, "Now, here, take this ten dollars and buy yourself some blue suede shoes. And next time, do not make the mistake of latching onto *my* pocketbook *nor nobody else's*—because shoes come by devilish like that will burn your feet. I got to get my rest now. But from here on in, son, I hope you will behave yourself."
>
> She led him down the hall to the front door and opened it. "Goodnight! Behave yourself, boy!" she said, looking out into the street as he went down the steps.
>
> The boy wanted to say something else other than "Thank you, m'am" to Mrs. Luella Bates Washington Jones, but although his lips moved, he couldn't even say that as he turned at the foot of the barren stoop and looked up at the large woman in the door. Then she shut the door.

After I finished, I said, "You know what to do. What thinking work is most interesting now? Turn and try it out."

While students talked, I noticed that many were finally thinking about the themes of the text. One partnership said, "I think it's about how being kind to others can have a lasting impact." Another said, "I think it's about how sometimes you can trust someone quickly."

I pulled them back to summarize. "Several of you tried a new kind of reading work. You thought about what themes this text *might* teach, what you, the reader, might be able to learn from it. Let's add that to our chart, because I bet that kind of thinking will pay off in other books you read." I added, "Relating lessons to our own lives" on a small Post-it and added it to the larger Post-it, "Considering lessons characters learn."

Soon, our chart looked like the one in Figure 20–3.

LINK

Ask students to try this work in the book they are reading or one they just finished—documenting the reading work that matters most, and what places in the book most invite that reading work.

"Fascinating! I'm taking a picture of this chart to document the work you've done. Right now, you have a few minutes to try this in your own books. Decide what reading work the book wants you to do, and mark the places in the book where it most invites that reading work. Then after a bit, you'll give each other tours of your books and the thinking work they invite.

"So now, take some blank Post-its. Jot a few of the thinking moves you already know your book invites. Then bring some blanks with you as well. You'll skim back over your book, and put these Post-its in the pages that most invite that work. Your book, like the story we just read, might invite new reading work.

"At the end of our reading time, take a few minutes to meet with your partner and compare your work. Work with the book you're reading now, or one you finished already. Also, you can work at your seats or you can stay here, if you would find it helpful to see the work we just did."

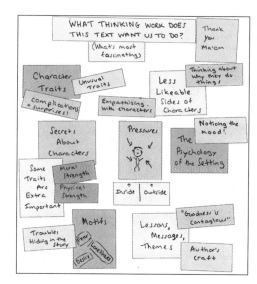

FIG. 20–3 The chart at the end of read-aloud work.

INDEPENDENT READING

Encouraging Metacognition in the Reading Process

As students work, circulate, first making sure they know what they are doing (skimming over their own books, inserting Post-its to mark the kind of thinking work the story invites). As they work, make a big deal of the work they are doing. Here are some quick comments you might make as you "lean in" over their shoulders.

> "Lean in" Comments to Build Student Energy for Independent Thinking
> - That's interesting, what part of the story invites that thinking?
> - Fascinating, I bet that comes up more than once.
> - Hmm, . . . that's intriguing. Is that thinking work especially significant in this book?
> - Hmm, . . . I've never really thought of that. I'll try that out in what I'm reading.
> - Oh, show that to . . . I think it might work in the book she's reading too.
> - I love how you're inventing some reading work.
> - That's fascinating. I wonder if it comes up again later.
> - How interesting. It makes me want to reread that part.

SHARE

Invite readers to give tours of the thinking work their story invites to each other.

"Readers, find a partner and give each other tours of the thinking work your story invites. Partners, ask for explanations. Give specific compliments. Notice if your partner is inventing new reading work, or applying reading work in interesting ways."

SESSION 20 HOMEWORK

DISCOVERING NEW THINKING WORK

Tonight, when you read, will you notice when your story seems to particularly suggest some important thinking work? Especially notice if the story seems to suggest thinking work we *haven't* done together as a class. Will you mark those passages with a Post-it, and on the Post-it, jot what that thinking work might be? For instance, if you notice that a character who you thought was good seems to become a villain, you might mark the exact spot where you began to think that, and on the Post-it write, "Noting when hidden villains emerge." As always, aim for your target minutes and pages, and log your reading.

Session 21

Reflection and Agency Centers

ear Teachers,

You did it! You set out to move your readers across an arc of closer reading, deeper thinking, more purposeful writing about reading, more literary conversation, and greater agency and independence. Now you and your readers are at the far shore, where you should rest for a moment.

Take a moment, this afternoon, as your readers move among centers (which you'll find out about in the following text), to listen to some of their conversations. Glance over their notebooks and their reading logs. As you do this, watch and listen to your students with the lens of "how is my teaching changing them?" It is. Some changes will be grand and visible. There will be kids who used to breeze through books, thinking about the plot, who now notice subtle details about characters. There will be partners who used to sit in torturous silence, eventually mumbling things like, "I think Katniss is scared," who now compare the parts of their characters that they find likeable and less so, and the pressures that help explain these parts. There will be a kid who wasn't really reading, who now is. That's a life-changing event, even if the kid doesn't know it yet. And there will be some that you are still worried about. It's the worrying about the few that makes you the teacher you are. Look, though, right now, at what you *have* accomplished, and hold onto the beauty of that, for to stay in teaching you must know how to hold onto beauty.

REFLECTION AND AGENCY CENTERS

Today, you'll invite your students to move through centers that are set up to invite reflection and agency. The resources for these centers are on the online resources, so take a moment to download and print them. You do need a little bit of technology. At one center, kids need to watch a video. At another they need to take a picture of a page from their notebook, or better yet, scan it using a scanner app. At a third they need to read a picture book together. If you duplicate these centers, then you need two of each of these items.

Materials for Centers

You need a few things for these centers:

- One or two tablets or computers with uploaded videos (see online resources for URLs)
- One or two smart phones, cameras, or other devices able to take photos, or even better, a scanner app
- Two to four picture books for teens (such as *Your Move* by Eve Bunting, *Riding the Tiger* by Eve Bunting, *Rose Blanche* by Roberto Innocente, *Patrol* by Walter Dean Myers). You may need to pencil in page numbers in the books.
- Center packets (available on the online resources)
- Post-its and markers
- There are four centers. Four students will be at a center at a time. Make as many copies of each as you need (for example, for thirty-two students, you'll need two copies of each so that you have eight centers), and set them out on tables.
- Set up a few extra centers, so if a group is ready to move on sooner, they may.

Your readers will need to travel through these centers with a few things:

- Reading partner
- Reading notebook
- Post-its
- Reading log (whatever form it is)
- Independent reading book(s)

You don't need to give a minilesson today. Instead, say something like, "Readers, you've grown in extraordinary ways as readers over the last few weeks. Today, you have a chance to reflect on that growth and demonstrate it. There are reflection and agency centers around the room. Each center has an activity that will lead you to reflect, to set goals, or to show agency and apply what you've learned.

"First, take a moment to gather the materials you'll need: your partner, your reading notebook, some Post-its, your reading log, and your book or books.

"The reflection centers will go pretty quickly—'The Notebook Museum' and 'Where Are You as a Reader?' Make sure you visit one of those today. The agency centers will take a little longer. Those are the 'Never Stop Thinking' and 'Student-Led Read-Aloud' centers, so choose just one of those. If you've done one agency center and a reflection center, then you can probably fit in a third.

"Once you have everything, off you go. I'll give you a heads-up at eight minutes or so, so you can begin to wrap up and get ready to move to a new center. That way, you're sure to visit at least two centers."

Agency Center 1
Never Stop Thinking—Applying Reading Strategies to a Digital Narrative

- Center packet
- Tablet or computer to play video

Reflection Center One
Where are You as a Reader? Giving Tours of Your Reading Lives

Welcome!

Here's what you need at this center:
- A reading partner
- Your reading log
- Your notebook, especially pages with any reading plans
- Courses of Study

Introduction
In this center you'll spend some time reflecting on your reading life by looking at artifacts such as your reading log and any reading plans you've made, thinking about what's going well and what's next for you. Then you'll give a tour of your reading life, using these artifacts. You'll talk about what books you've read, how you chose them, how reading has been going, and your plans for what's next.

Some tips:
- Be honest about when things went well, and when they didn't.
- Listen to your partner, study your partner's artifacts, and give honest advice.
- Study your partner's data like a scientist. Be analytical. Notice patterns, consider cause & effect relationships.
- Be innovative in how you problem solve. Don't stop with easy solutions, think about what might really help in the long term.

Step 1
First, study the data from your reading log with the lens of volume and rate. Really try to analyze this data. When are you getting the most reading done? Why? Is your reading rate stable or does it vary depending on the book? What about your volume? How often are you in a reading zone (40-60 pages across the whole day)?

Step 2
Compare with your partner. How is reading going? How satisfied are you with your volume and rate of reading? What tips can you give each other?

Step 3
Still looking at your reading logs, tell each other a bit about how you chose your books. Have your Courses of Study, and any reading plans you've made next to you as well, and talk about what kinds of books you've been trying to read, and how your personal Course of Study is helping you grow as a reader.

Step 4
Wrap up by giving each other compliments and tips. Think about what might be next for each of you.

Reflection Center Two
The Notebook Museum

Welcome!

Here's what you need at this center:
- A reading partner
- Your reading notebook
- Colored pencils and pens
- Your favorite book(s)
- Post-its
- An iPad or iPhone with a scanner app – or any way to scan
- Access to our class google drive or shared folder on a laptop

Introduction
In this center, you'll reflect on your reading notebook, choosing two or three pages to contribute to our Notebook Museum. You'll have time to do any revision to your notebook pages, to talk with a partner about which ones you want to share, and then to scan and upload these pages to our shared folder. You can also look at the pages your classmates have uploaded.

Step 1
First, take a few minutes to get your reading notebook ready. You might do some final revision or additions to a page. Then, look back over your reading notebook and to put Post-its on some favorite pages. You might choose two pages that show how much your writing about reading has changed and grown, or you might choose favorite pages that reflect your best work.

Step 2
Explain to your partner why you chose these two pages. Invite each other to consider other pages as well, and narrow your choices to the two or three pages you want to upload to our Notebook Museum. You can also study the pages classmates have uploaded.

Step 3
Using the iPhone, iPad, or other scanner app, scan in your pages and upload them to our shared file. Once they are uploaded, check to see that they are clear, and give them a title (such as 'Tracing motifs in *Hunger Games*').

Step 4
We'll also nominate 'Best in Show' pages. Study the pages that classmates have uploaded, and use a Post-it to nominate 'Best in Show.' Leave the Post-it in the folder for this center. You may want to check back later, as other classmates will have posted new pages.

FIG. 21–1 Centers engage students in working independently. Meanwhile, you can circulate and research students' skills, growth, and confidence.

Agency Center 2
Student-Led Read-Aloud

- Center packet
- Picture books
- Post-its

Reflection Center 1
Where Are You as a Reader? Giving Tours of Your Reading Life

- Center packet
- Courses of study handout
- Students' reading logs

Reflection Center 2
The Notebook Museum

- Center packet
- Smart phone, camera, or other device to take pictures or scan notebook pages

As your students engage with these centers, remember, this is your time to reflect as well. Listen in. Jot exact things they say for you to think about later. Carry your smart phone and video-record some conversations. Invite a colleague in to co-research the kids, and the unit, and your teaching, and how it's all going. Let kids know that as they research their growth, you'll be researching them, striving to document evidence of their powers. If you look ahead at the final portion of this letter, about "thin-slicing" to study student data, you'll see that you may want to choose three students, and video-record or jot notes about their work in particular.

At the end of the period, after you've tasked students to finish at their centers and return the tools for other students to use, gather them to take a final moment to reflect and celebrate. You might say, "Readers, I'm going to be watching some of these videos and looking at my notes, and you might want to do the same. Watch a story with a friend, or someone in your family, and share some of the things you see in it. Or read aloud to a sibling—you might use a picture book like the ones we used today. I have some you can sign out for an evening.

"To finish, today, and this unit, will you do one thing? Will you tell your partner what are you most happy about, in terms of your reading growth? Is it the work you did just now? Is it that you are in slightly harder books? Is it better partner work? Is it more reading? Take a moment to reflect, and then tell your partner. Then think . . . how will you hold onto this work?"

Then . . . send your readers off.

WRAPPING UP FOR YOU, INCLUDING STUDYING STUDENT DATA

There are a few things that I often do at the end of a unit that you might consider.

- I take down all the teaching charts, and I consider making mini-versions of them, to put in a reading center, or to paste into notebooks. Well, to be clear, I don't make them myself; I invite some students to make mini-versions for the class.

- I take stock of the library, and consider what we can do to make it even more inviting, to organize it in ways that lead readers to follow up on authors, series, and genres, and how we can fill in gaps and get new books in. I buy used books, I beg for books, I put out letters to friends and parents, I talk to kids about getting books.

- I thin-slice my data so I can reflect on responsiveness to teaching and student growth. It's not really possible for a middle school teacher to study all student work deeply—you just have too much student work to do that. Thin-slicing helps you study student data deeply. To do this, I choose three students whose work will represent groups of students. Usually, a "typical" student whose work represents most of the class, a student whose work represents my strongest readers, and a student who represents readers who read below grade level. I take these three students' reading logs and reading notebooks, and I study them deeply, noting the work they were doing at the start of the unit and throughout the unit. Often, I have my teaching points or anchor charts next to me, and I specifically look for evidence of those teaching points in student work. From this analysis, I have an evidence-based theory for how students have grown, how they are responding to instruction, and what work they may still struggle with or avoid.

Remember to share what you find, and the work students have done, with teachers, families, and your administration. You need to be a change agent! If you see your students becoming more powerful close readers, if they care about books more, if they read more, if they are affected by what they read, invite colleagues and families into your research. Call parents and let them know how their kids are growing. Put up a wall, outside the classroom, of pages from your notebook museum. Ask kids to donate annotated texts to the classroom library. And . . . tonight, raise a glass to yourself, and the work you've done. You've initiated teens into the reading club.

All the best,
Mary